IMAGES
of America

LYNN

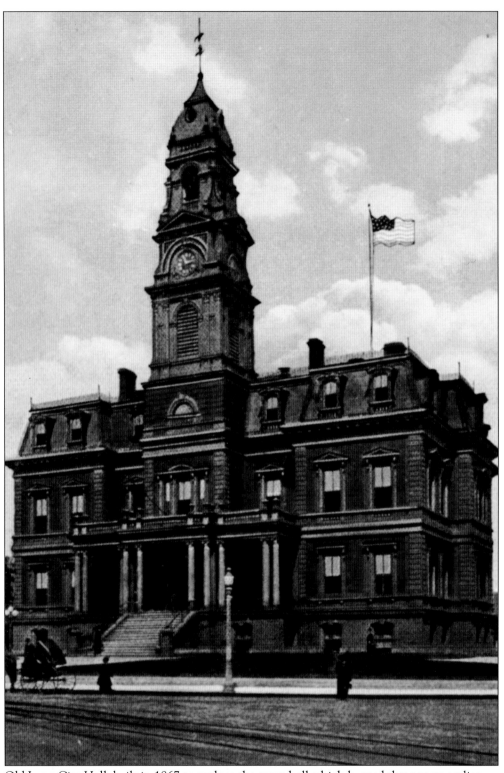

Old Lynn City Hall, built in 1867 to replace the town hall which burned three years earlier.

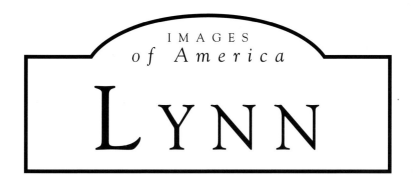

IMAGES
of America

LYNN

Joanne S. Foley

ARCADIA
PUBLISHING

Copyright © 1995 by Joanne S. Foley
ISBN 978-0-7385-7241-3

Published by Arcadia Publishing
Charleston SC, Chicago IL, Portsmouth NH, San Francisco CA

Printed in the United States of America

Library of Congress Catalog Card Number: 2009934190

For all general information contact Arcadia Publishing at:
Telephone 843-853-2070
Fax 843-853-0044
E-mail sales@arcadiapublishing.com
For customer service and orders:
Toll-Free 1-888-313-2665

Visit us on the Internet at www.arcadiapublishing.com

Dedication

To Lynn's industrious pioneers of the past
and to those of the present who carry on the traditions.

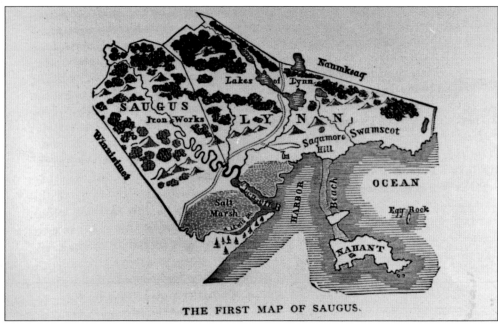

THE FIRST MAP OF SAUGUS.

The first map of Saugus and Lynn.

CONTENTS

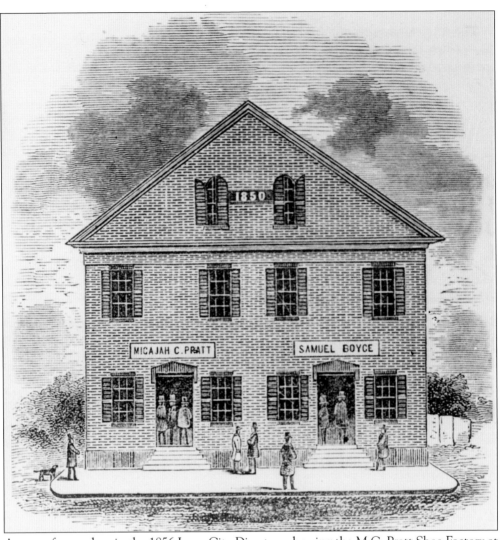

A copy of a woodcut in the 1856 Lynn City Directory showing the M.C. Pratt Shoe Factory at 98 Broad Street and the Samuel Boyce Shoe Factory at 100 Broad Street.

INTRODUCTION

Lynn was first settled in 1629 under the Indian name of Saugus, but in 1637 the name was changed to Lynn after King's Lynn in England. It is one of the oldest towns in Massachusetts, the original tract of land including the present towns of Swampscott, Nahant, Saugus, Lynnfield, and part of Reading. Situated on the north shore of Massachusetts Bay, Lynn is 10 miles north of Boston and 5 miles south of Salem. Poet and historian Alonzo Lewis once described it as "a region of romance and beauty" that extended from its beaches and craggy cliffs back to rocky hills and woods of evergreen.

Early settlers in Lynn brought with them the skills needed for the beginnings of the shoe industry, which would become a burgeoning business in the next century. In 1750 Welsh immigrant John Adam Dagyr, known for his ability to produce high-quality ladies shoes, came to Lynn, and shortly thereafter the city gained a reputation for being a leading manufacturer of shoes. The year 1838 marked the coming of the first steam railroad, which opened new possibilities for Lynn as a manufacturing town. The McKay sewing machine pioneered the great change from handmade to factory systems in ten years time, beginning in 1861 with the making of army brogans. With the changes in shoe production came the beginning of the labor unions. The St. Crispin organization, formed in Lynn, was probably the largest in the country. The Great Fire of 1889 devastated much of the area's business district; however, the city soon rose again from the ashes with renewed vigor.

During this period of manufacturing growth, other things were happening in the city. Earlier in the century an engineering milestone was passed in 1804 when the first pontoon bridge in the country was constructed over Collins Pond, the bridge we know today as the "Floating Bridge." This was built at the time of construction of the turnpike between Salem and Boston (Western Avenue), and tolls were collected until the costs were paid off. The turnpike project marked one of the greatest steps in the progress of Lynn and its relations with other communities.

Women were prominent in Lynn's history in the nineteenth century as Lydia Pinkham became the first successful, and best known, businesswoman in the country. Lydia Pinkham's "Vegetable Compound" became familiar all over the world as a medicine for "female complaints." Maria Mitchell, a brilliant astronomer, discovered a comet, and Mary Baker Eddy founded the Christian Science faith. Women's suffrage issues were popular at that time, and women began to pursue their rights as well as fight for other causes, such as abolitionism.

The year 1883 brought Lynn a new industry, that of electrical products. Ten years later the General Electric Company emerged and contributed much to the prosperity of the city. The same year also brought the opening of the Lynn Hospital on Boston Street.

Many were the legends of Lynn in the early days. Hiram Marble settled in Lynn Woods at Dungeon Rock, and spent the remainder of his life digging for the treasure the pirate Thomas Veal was supposed to have buried there. He financed his venture by selling shares for $1. The members of the Hutchinson family, all staunch abolitionists, purchased High Rock and often entertained people there with their patriotic songs. Moll Pitcher, renowned for her fortune telling, was sought out by people from all walks of life.

The photographs in this book have been selected to illustrate Lynn's unique and colorful history of the past, and are gathered with the hope that they will be a source of enjoyment to all, young and old, who read this book.

One

THE HEART OF LYNN

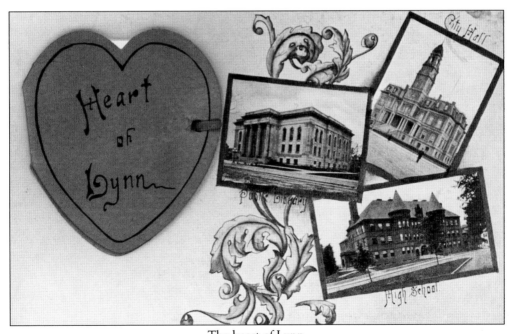

The heart of Lynn.

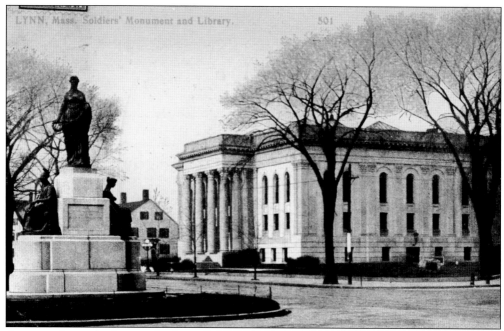

A postcard view looking at the Lynn Public Library and the Soldiers' Monument. The public library, a fine example of Renaissance Revival architecture, opened for use in April 1900. A bequest to the City of Lynn from Mrs. Elizabeth M. Shute, in memory of her late husband William Shute, was left for the purpose of constructing a library.

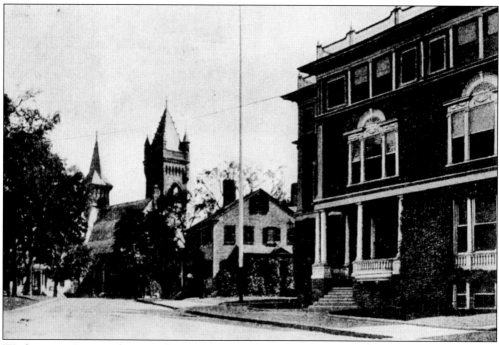

Washington Square, showing the Oxford Club (right) and the First Universalist Church on Nahant Street (further down the road). The Oxford Clubhouse was built in 1892 and was a popular place for men to socialize.

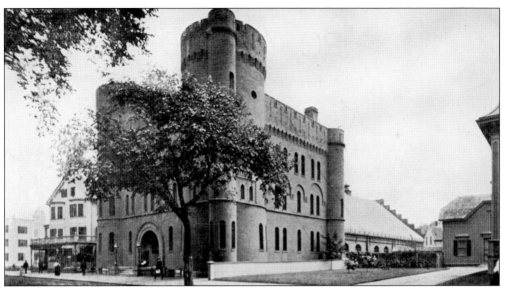

A *c.* 1907 postcard view of the Commonwealth Armory, built on South Common Street in 1893.

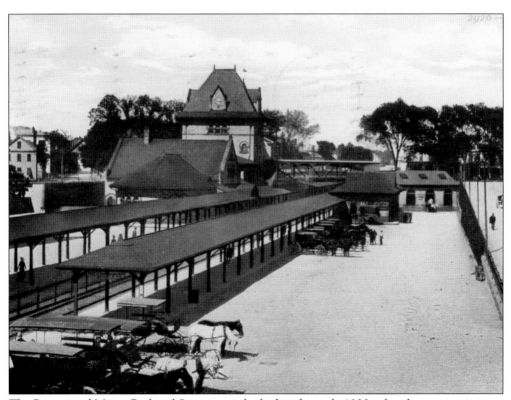

The Boston and Maine Railroad Station as it looked in the early 1900s after the new station was built. The horses with their wagons and carriages are lined up waiting for the train to come in.

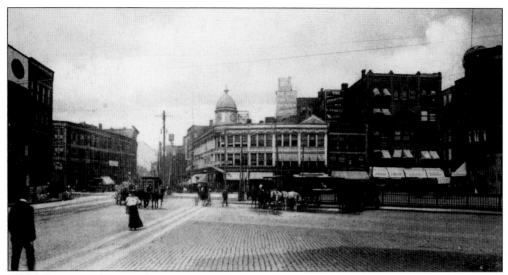

Central Square, showing the Security Trust Co. (center) and the Johnson Co. clothiers (the large building to the right). This photograph was taken c. 1905.

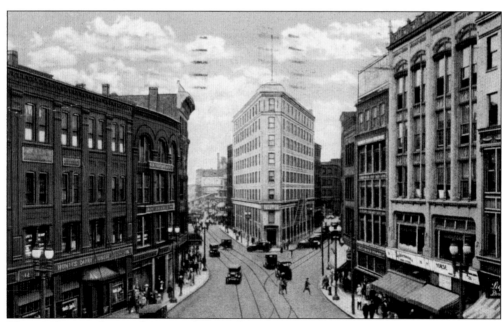

This 1928 view of Central Square shows a change in the mode of transportation, as cars have replaced all the horses and wagons.

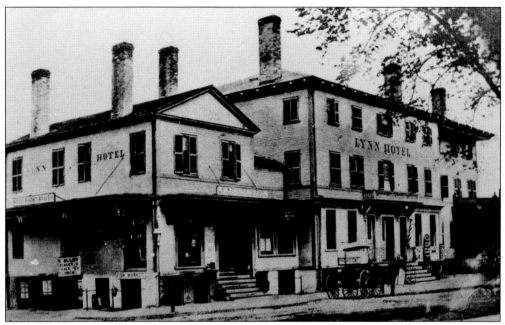

The Lynn Hotel was built in 1803 at the time of the opening of the turnpike between Salem and Boston (Western Avenue), and served as a popular stagecoach stop and tavern. It was said to be the first three-story building erected in Lynn. Lafayette Hall was on the second floor and served as a meeting hall for a number of organizations. During the development of the bicycle, the first school of instruction was begun here. (Courtesy of the Mount Carmel Lodge.)

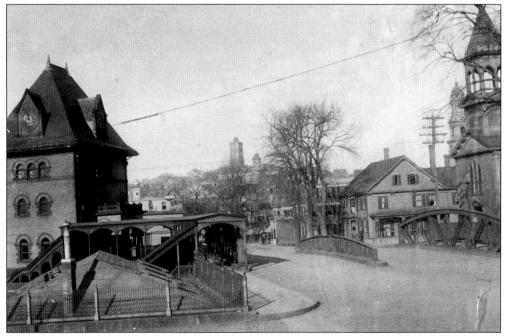

This view, from the corner of Mt. Vernon Street, looks north along Silsbee Street and across the bridge over the Boston & Maine train tracks. In the distance is the High Rock Tower. (Photo courtesy of the Lynn, MA Public Library.)

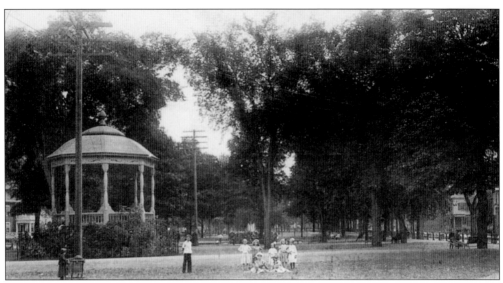

A group of children playing on Lynn Common near the bandstand.

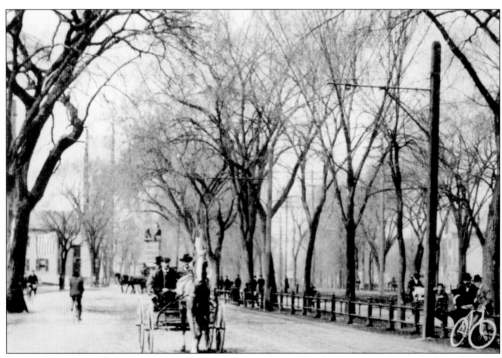

Simon Weinberger's horse and carriage traveling down South Common Street. Note the men and their bicycles leaning against the iron fence. The fence, which surrounded the entire common, was installed in 1878. (Courtesy of the North Shore Jewish Historical Society.)

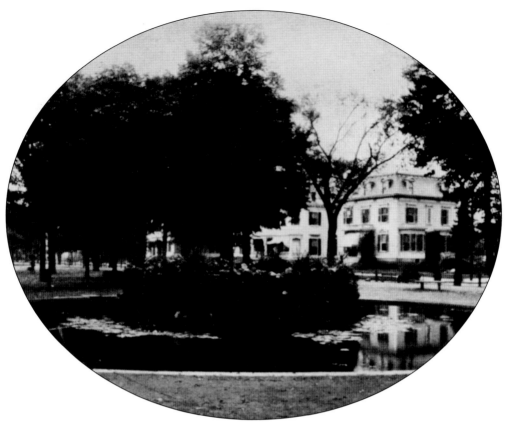

A pleasant view of the electric fountain and Frog Pond on Lynn Common. The 1891 bequest of William Shute provided for a lighted electric fountain in Frog Pond. (Courtesy of the North Shore Jewish Historical Society.)

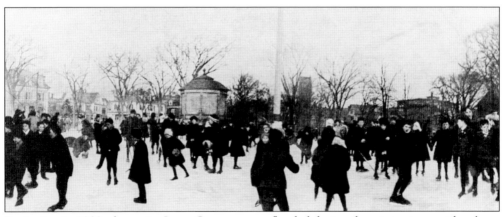

Beginning in 1903, the entire Lynn Common was flooded during the winter to provide a large recreation area for skaters, and a skating carnival was held there each year. Skaters crowd the ice in this photograph taken January 20, 1908. (Photo courtesy of the Lynn, MA Public Library.)

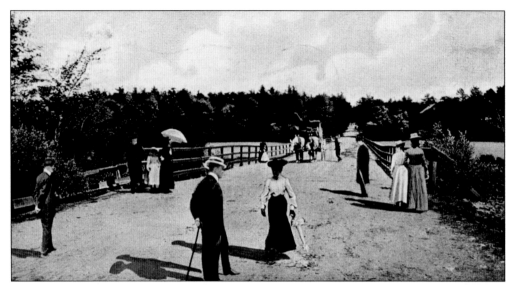

The Floating Bridge, or Buchanen Bridge, was built over Collin's Pond in 1804 at the time of the construction of the turnpike between Boston and Salem. It was over 500 feet in length and actually floated on the water. When this photograph was taken in the early 1900s, the bridge was already over a hundred years old.

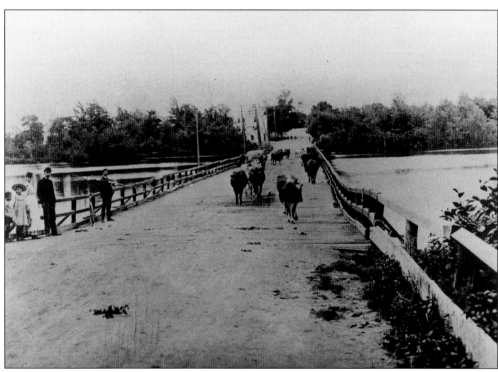

Although the Floating Bridge was a favorite place for a stroll or carriage ride, cows were often seen crossing the bridge as well. (Courtesy of Martha Lewis.)

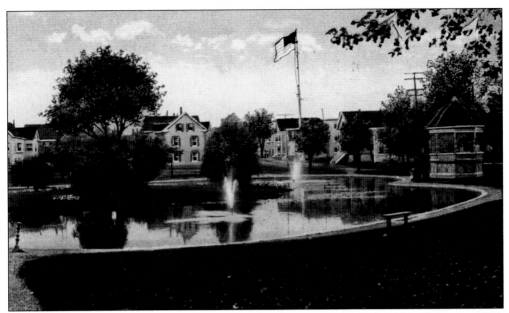

A serene, scenic view of Lafayette Park and Goldfish Pond in the early 1900s. Begun in 1870, the park was a favorite recreational spot for people in the area.

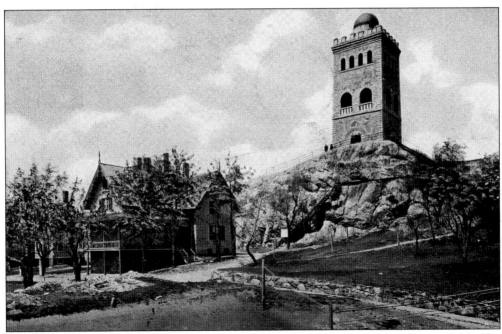

An early view of the High Rock Tower and Hutchinson's Stone Cottage (to the left). The Stone Cottage was built by Jesse Hutchinson from granite quarried on his property, but it was not until many years later, in 1905, that the High Rock Tower was completed.

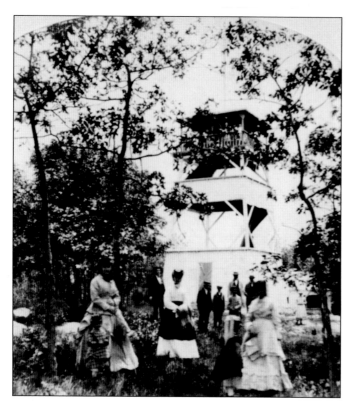

This stereoscopic view shows people dressed up for a picnic party at Echo Grove in Lynn Woods. Echo Grove was located on the western slope of Tower Hill, and after 1880 it became an important meeting place for Lynn's spiritualists, whose weekly gatherings included speakers, instrumental music, and demonstrations by mediums.

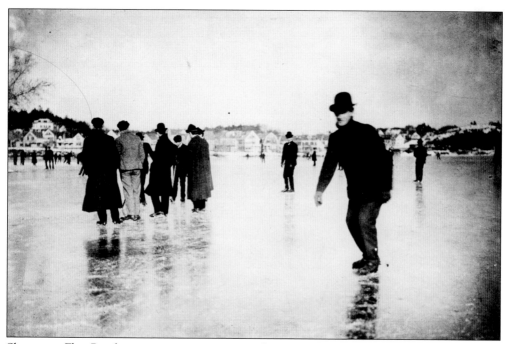

Skaters on Flax Pond enjoying some exercise and conversation. Note the hats and long coats. (Courtesy of the Peabody Essex Museum, Salem, MA.)

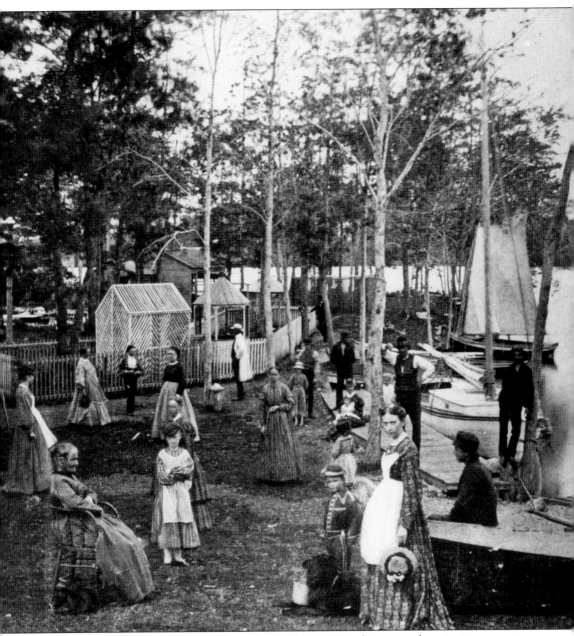

This wonderful old stereoview, possibly taken in the 1880s, shows people enjoying a respite on the shores of Flax Pond. Sailing was a popular summer sport, as this photograph indicates. (Courtesy of the Peabody Essex Museum, Salem, MA.)

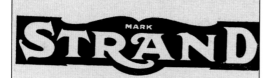

MARK

STRAND

ᔕ"The Theatre Beautiful"ᔐ

Clean, Artistic and Entertaining

Photo Plays

PROPERLY PRESENTED WITH

High-Class Music

Clean Entertainment is as Essential to Healthy Living as Pure Water

The Strand Theatre, "The Theatre Beautiful," had been in business for twelve years when this 1927 ad was printed.

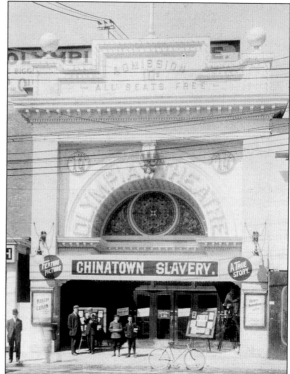

The Olympia Theatre was located just off Olympia Square. It had two balconies, with an escalator to the first balcony, which was reported to be the first escalator in Lynn. (Photo courtesy of the Lynn, MA Public Library.)

The Mark Comique was a vaudeville theatre that charged only 10¢ "to see it all." Old timers remember going there to see cowboy pictures with "cliff-hanger" scenes, which meant that you had to come back next week to see what happened. Blackstone the Magician was also a favorite entertainer at the Comique. Today, Beden Hardware is located at the site where the Mark Comique once stood. (Courtesy of the Lynn, MA Public Library.)

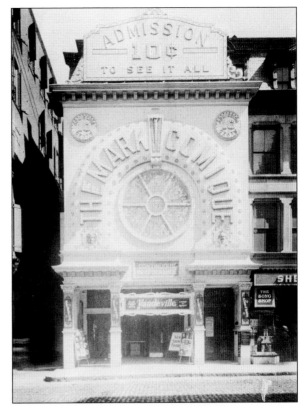

The Strand Theatre celebrated its 5th anniversary on November 29, 1920. (Courtesy of the St. Stephens Episcopal Church.)

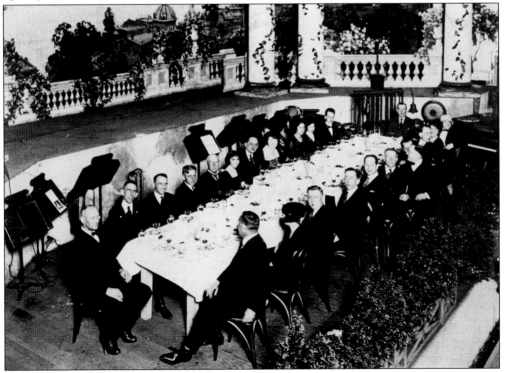

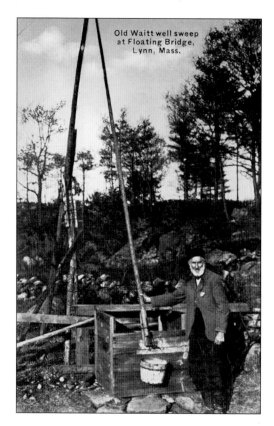

A postcard view of Old Waitt, a well sweep at the Floating Bridge.

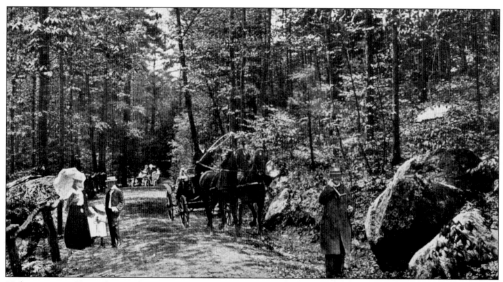

Taking a stroll or drive along Dungeon Rock Road was a popular pastime for Lynn residents. Note the early car in the background.

Two

STREETS AND BUSINESSES

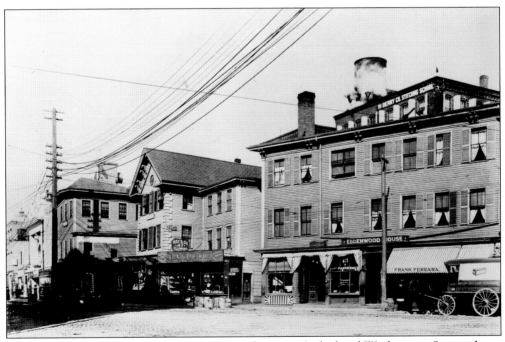

Olympia Square. This view of Central Avenue between Oxford and Washington Streets shows Frank Ferrera's fruit and confectionery store. At 47 Central Avenue is L.A. May & Co., who were in the plumbing and heating business for over thirty years. To the far left is the Olympia Theatre, and peering above it all is the Berry Co. Stitching School. (Photo courtesy of the Lynn, MA Public Library.)

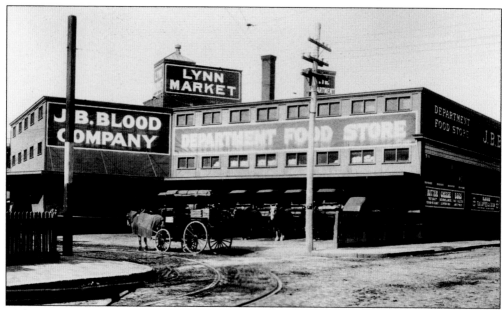

The J.B. Blood Co. This 1910 photograph shows the back of J.B. Blood's department food store, with horses and delivery wagons lined up waiting to make deliveries throughout the city. The largest grocery store in Lynn, the J.B Blood Co. was located on Summer Street at the corner of Pleasant, and dealt in all lines and varieties of foods, teas and coffees, and kitchen furnishings. (Phto courtesy of the Lynn, MA Public Library.)

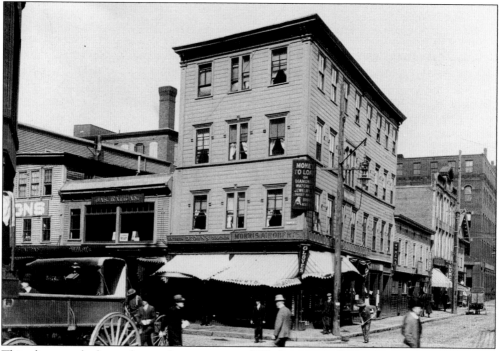

This photograph shows the northwest corner of Washington and Munroe Streets on a typical business day. Note the street cleaner in the foreground. (Photo courtesy of the Lynn, MA Public Library.)

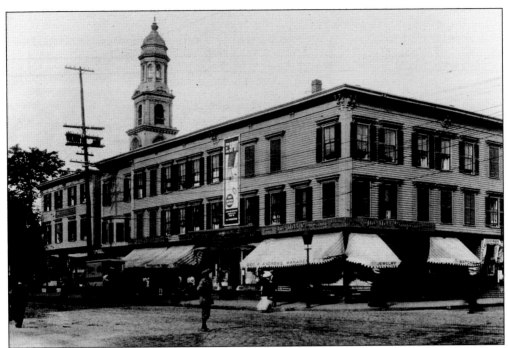

Freeman Square. The spire of the East Baptist Church overlooks businesses in Freeman Square at the comer of Union and Silsbee Streets. This photograph was taken about 1911. (Photo courtesy of the Lynn, MA Public Library.)

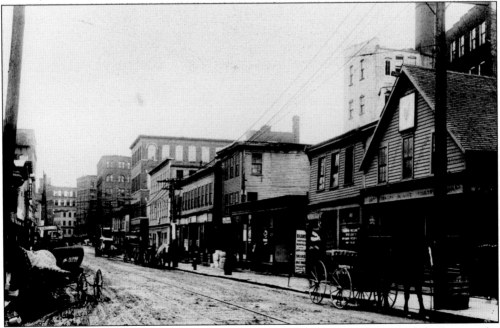

Horses and buggies line both sides of the street in this Wentworth photograph looking at the south side of Oxford Street, from Orleans and Chambers to Washington Street. The store on the right deals in "live poultry" and advertises with a picture of a chicken at the top of the building. (Photo courtesy of the Lynn, MA Public Library.)

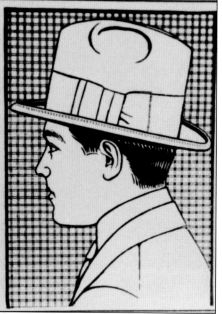

RIGHT GOODS   FAIR PRICES

The New Fall Styles

Beroco Hats

Now Ready

THE SNAPPIEST LINE FOR YOUNG MEN

$1.45 $2 $3

BESSE=ROLFE CO.

Say BEROCO!   Say it Plain!!

Beroco Hats were "snappy" hats for young men in 1915.

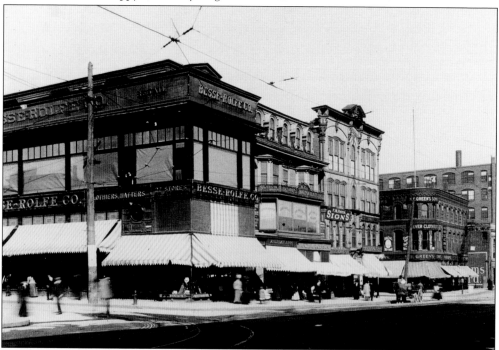

The Besse-Rolfe Co. was in business for many years. Located at the corner of Market and Oxford Streets, they advertised as clothiers, hatters, and outfitters, but also sold boots and shoes. This 1910 photograph shows the east side of Market Street from Oxford to the Boston and Maine Railroad. (Photo courtesy of the Lynn, MA Public Library.)

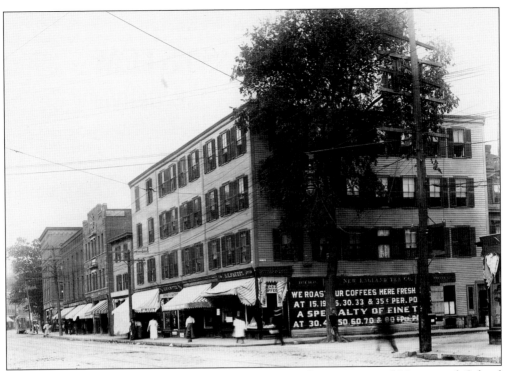

The New England Tea Company, located at the northeast corner of Union and School Streets, advertises its wares on the side of the building for everyone to see. (Courtesy of the Atlanticare Hospital.)

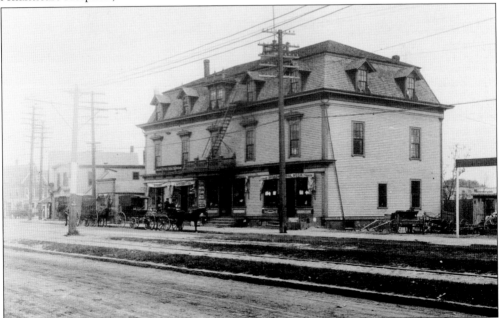

A view of Broadway in Wyoma Square, showing the Wyoma Grocery Co. with horses and delivery wagons outside. At the other end of the building is the Broadway Pool Room. (Photo courtesy of the Lynn, MA Public Library.)

Your Attention is Called to the

COUPON SYSTEM
of the North Shore Ice Delivery Co.

It is strongly recommended because it ensures the
lowest price and gives you perfect control of your

ICE CONSUMPTION

Pure Certified Ice Delivered in Lynn, Swampscott and Nahant
and the Best of Service Guaranteed

Respectfully Yours,

North Shore Ice Delivery Co.

46 Lake Avenue   Lynn, Mass.

Telephone   Jackson   703-557-698

A 1926 advertisement recommending the North Shore Ice Delivery Company's "Coupon System."

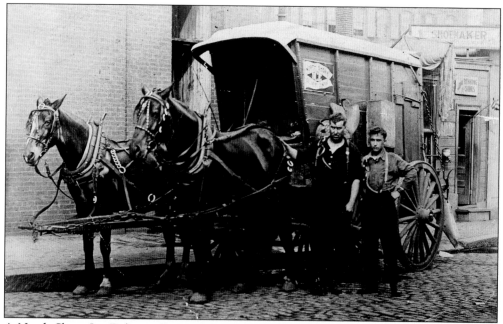

A North Shore Ice Delivery Company wagon remains parked by the side of the road, while owner Warren Tinkham and his son Warren Jr. take time out for a picture. The Ice Company was in business for many years serving people in Lynn, Swampscott, and Nahant. (Courtesy of Roger Tinkham.)

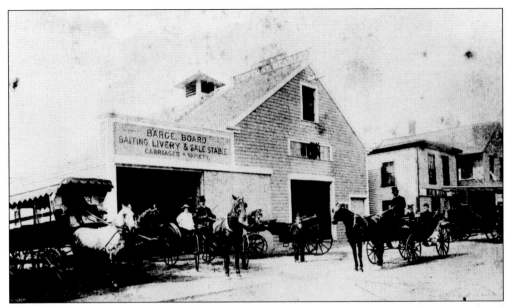

The Goodell stables at the corner of Summer Street and Willow Road in Nahant rented and stalled horses and livery. In the left of the picture is one of the horse-drawn barges that carried residents and tourists between Lynn and Nahant, while in front of the building are the different types of carriages and landaus that were available for use by the residents of the area. Byron Goodell, owner of the stables, stands in center of the picture, with Mrs. Goodell seated on the right in the carriage. (Courtesy of the Nahant Historical Society.)

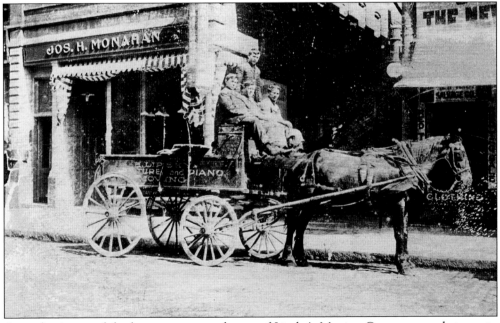

An early picture of the horse, wagon, and crew of Lipsky's Moving Company, ready to go to a moving job. The company is still in business today. (Courtesy of the North Shore Jewish Historical Society.)

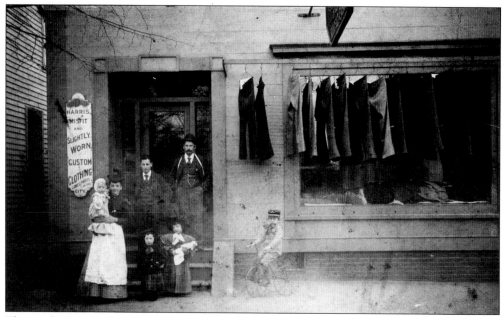

This is the Harris family standing outside their store on Munroe Street in 1892. The store advertises misfit, slightly worn, and custom clothing. Note the row of pants hanging on the right. (Courtesy of the North Shore Jewish Historical Society.)

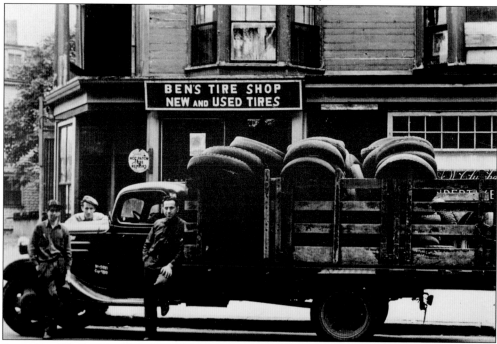

Ben's Tire Shop opened in Lynn about 1930 and was a local landmark for sixty-two years. Pictured on the right is the owner, Benjamin Stone. He emigrated from Poland at age seven, and by age twelve was working in a shoe factory, earning $2 a week. He learned the tire business from his brother-in-law in Maine, and later returned to Lynn to start his own business. (Courtesy of the North Shore Jewish Historical Society.)

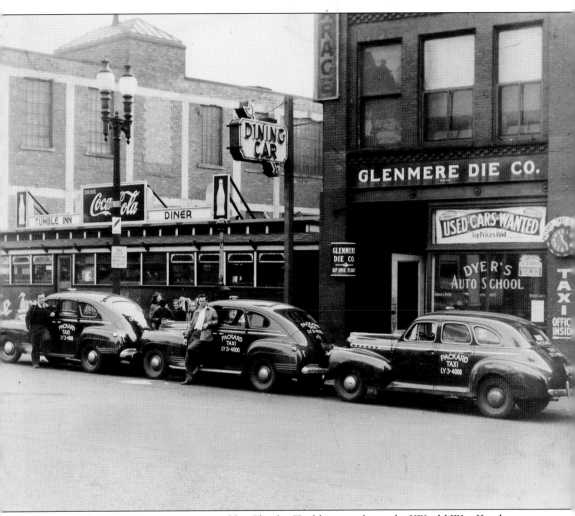

The Packard Taxi Company was started by Charles Tinkham at the end of World War II, when he returned from a tour of duty in Europe as General Eisenhower's personal chauffeur. It was located on Broad Street next to the Glenmere Die Co. and the Tumble Inn Diner. Later, when Charles Tinkham was co-owner of the company, it became known as Tom's Taxi. (Courtesy of Roger Tinkham.)

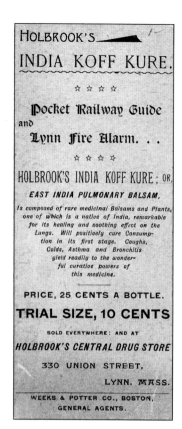

HOLBROOK'S

INDIA KOFF KURE.

☆ ☆ ☆ ☆

Pocket Railway Guide
and
Lynn Fire Alarm. . .

☆ ☆ ☆ ☆

HOLBROOK'S INDIA KOFF KURE; OR,

EAST INDIA PULMONARY BALSAM,

Is composed of rare medicinal Balsams and Plants,
one of which is a native of India, remarkable
for its healing and soothing effect on the
Lungs. Will positively cure Consump-
tion in its first stage. Coughs,
Colds, Asthma and Bronchitis
yield readily to the wonderful curative powers of
this medicine.

PRICE, 25 CENTS A BOTTLE.

TRIAL SIZE, 10 CENTS

SOLD EVERYWHERE: AND AT

HOLBROOK'S CENTRAL DRUG STORE

330 UNION STREET,

LYNN, MASS.

WEEKS & POTTER CO., BOSTON,
GENERAL AGENTS.

Holbrook's Central Drug Store, located at 330 Union Street on Central Square, advertised its "INDIA KOFF KURE" by way of the *Lynn Fire Alarm and Pocket Railway Guide.* This handy little guide included time tables for the Narrow Gauge and main line trains, the electric cars from Central Square, and fire alarm box numbers as well.

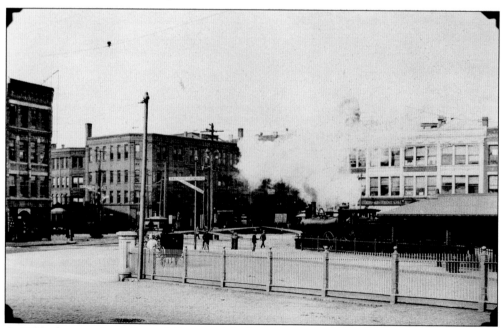

A 1899 photograph of Central Square with the train stopped at the station, belching forth steam from its stack. (Courtesy of the Atlanticare Hospital.)

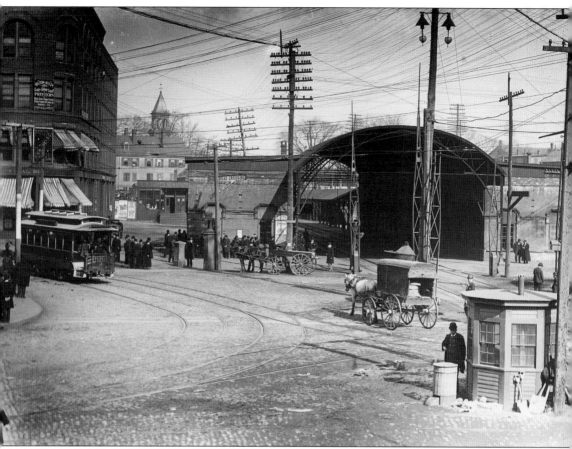

The Boston & Maine Railroad Station in Central Square after the Great Fire of 1889. This photograph was taken in 1893. The station was later rebuilt in 1897. (Courtesy of the Atlanticare Hospital.)

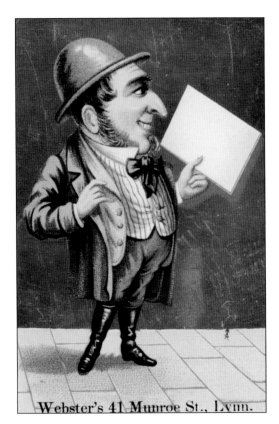

Webster's 41 Munroe St., Lynn.

In the 1880s and '90s merchants' advertising cards were popular. They were colorful and often whimsical advertisements, such as this card from Webster's at 41 Munroe Street. Eben Webster and his brother Charles ran the store, which sold men's clothes, boots, and shoes.

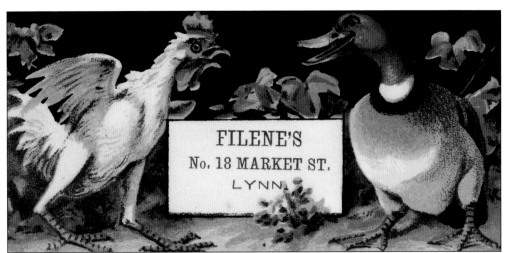

FILENE'S
No. 18 MARKET ST.
LYNN.

William Filene opened his first store in Salem in 1856 on Essex Street, selling clothing and dry goods. In 1861 he moved to Boston, and before 1880 he opened another store on Market Street in Lynn.

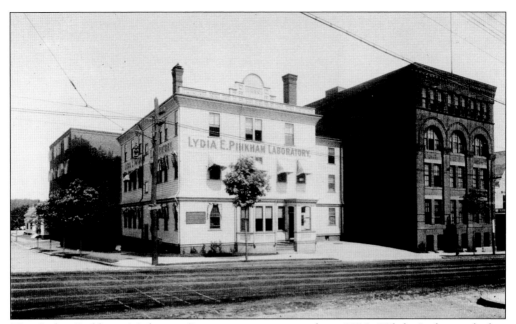

The Lydia Pinkham Medicine Company was organized in 1876. While Lydia made her famous Vegetable Compound, the rest of the family managed the business. Several years later it was decided to use a picture of Lydia Pinkham in their advertising and, as sales increased dramatically, Lydia Pinkham's name and face became a household word. (Photo courtesy of the Lynn, MA Public Library.)

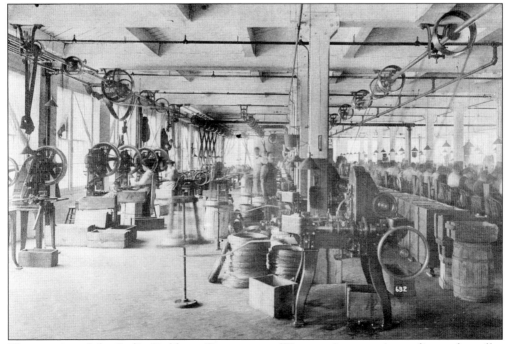

The interior of the Lydia Pinkham Company on Western Avenue. An earlier and smaller factory had been located a short distance away on the same street. (Courtesy of the Peabody Essex Museum, Salem, MA.)

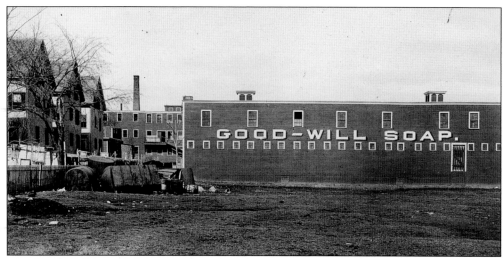

The Good Will Soap Works was first started by George E. Marsh. George, later joined by his brother, Caleb W. Marsh, eventually built a thriving business dealing in tallow and soap stock. In 1880 they advertised that "orders by mail or Express promptly attended to." The greatly expanding business necessitated moving to a larger site and in 1890 Good Will Soap moved to a new location on Chestnut Street. Lynn residents bringing in 100 pounds of bones to be used in soap making were rewarded with a shiny red cart to help bring in even larger amounts. This photograph of the factory on Chestnut Street was taken in 1911, just a year before the unfortunate death of George E. Marsh, who was killed by a relative in a dispute over family financial matters. (Courtesy of the Peabody Essex Museum, Salem, MA.)

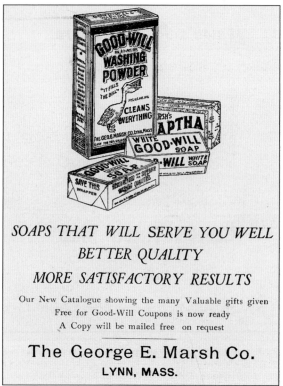

The George E. Marsh Company remained in business for some time after the death of Mr. Marsh, as evidenced by this 1926 advertisement.

Three

INDUSTRY

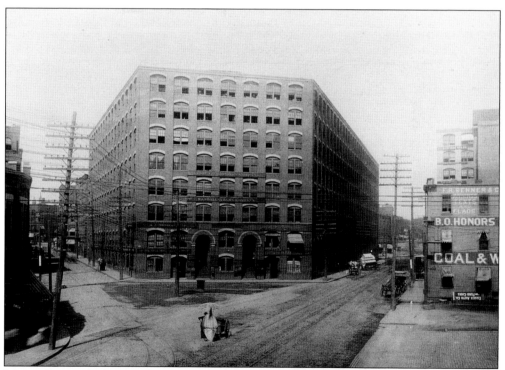

Liberty Square, looking at the Vamp Building. This building once had the distinction of being the largest shoe factory in the world; today, it is home to a number of Lynn's residents. Note the peanut vendor in the center foreground of the picture. (Photo courtesy of the Lynn, MA Public Library.)

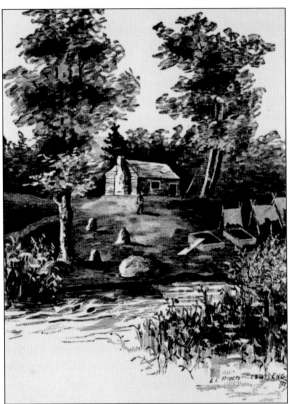

An illustration of the Ingalls log cabin, the site of the first tannery in New England in 1632. Francis Ingalls, Lynn's first recorded tanner, and his brother Edmund were two of the first settlers of the town.

Originally called Hammersmith, the Saugus Iron Works began on the banks of the Saugus River about 1643 and became the first successful ironworks in the country. Production continued here for about forty years. This view is of the reconstructed site of the Saugus Iron Works, seen from across the Saugus River. Finished in 1953, the site became part of the National Park System in 1969. (Courtesy of the Saugus Public Library.)

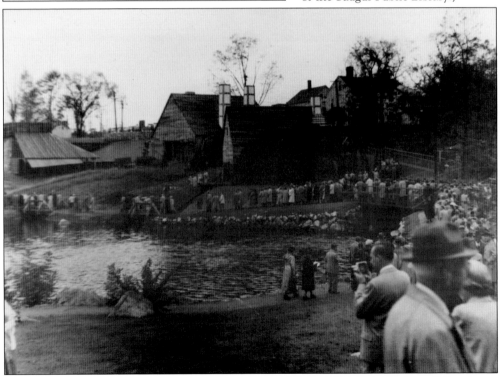

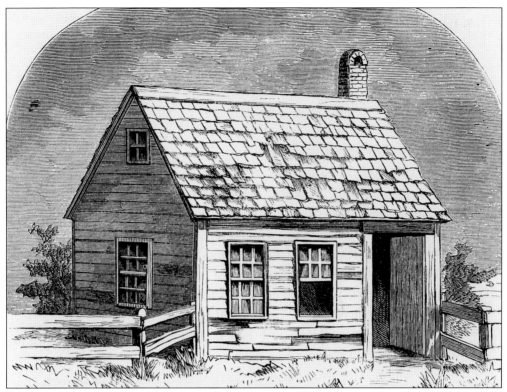

An illustration of a typical "ten-footer," the earliest of "shoe factories" in Lynn. These small square buildings were where Lynn's shoe business began, and were located near their owner's houses. Often the whole family was involved in the manufacture of shoes.

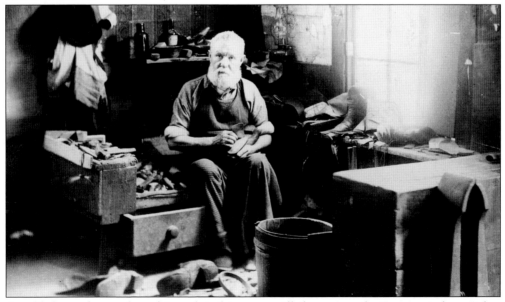

An old shoemaker works at his craft in his own small shop, part of a "cottage industry" that survived for many years until shoemaking gradually grew into a burgeoning factory business. (Courtesy of the Atlanticare Hospital.)

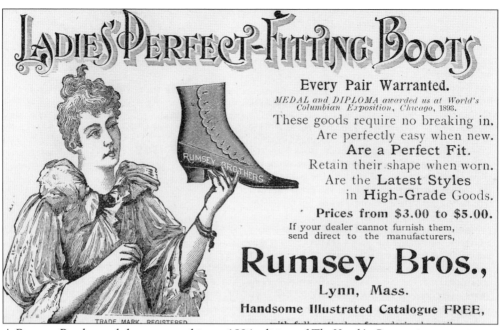

LADIES' PERFECT-FITTING BOOTS

Every Pair Warranted.

MEDAL and DIPLOMA awarded us at World's Columbian Exposition, Chicago, 1893.

These goods require no breaking in.

Are perfectly easy when new.

Are a Perfect Fit.

Retain their shape when worn.

Are the **Latest Styles** in **High-Grade** Goods.

Prices from $3.00 to $5.00.

If your dealer cannot furnish them, send direct to the manufacturers,

Rumsey Bros.,

Lynn, Mass.

Handsome Illustrated Catalogue FREE,

RUMSEY BROTHERS

TRADE MARK. REGISTERED

A Rumsey Brothers ad that appeared in an 1894 edition of *The Youth's Companion* magazine.

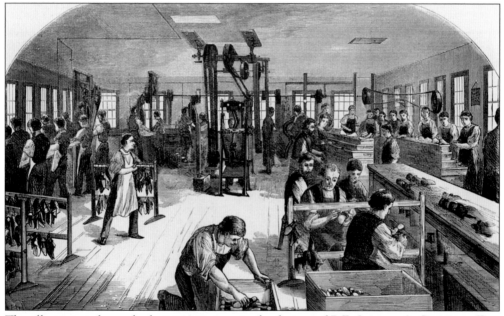

This illustration shows the bottoming room in the factory of B.F. Spinney & Company. First located on Willow Street, the business moved to a larger, newly-constructed building on Union Street in 1864. B.F. Spinney had a reputation for manufacturing "first class goods" and made a specialty of "ladies wear."

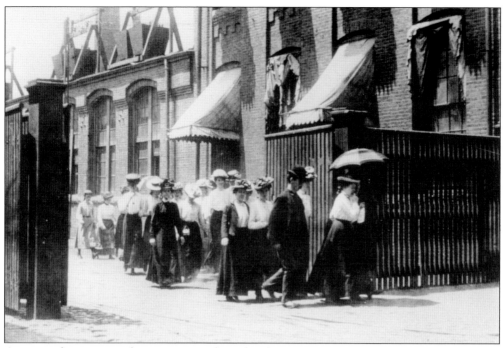

A group of women on their way to work in the shoe factory, looking dressed up and wearing their hats. (Courtesy of the North Shore Jewish Historical Society.)

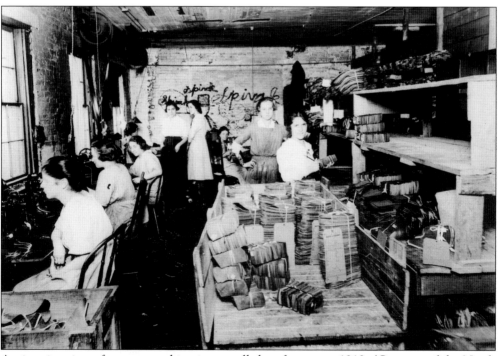

An interior view of women working in a small shoe factory, c. 1919. (Courtesy of the North Shore Jewish Historical Society.)

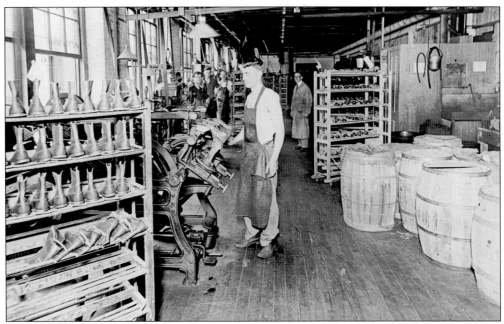

The Burdett Shoe Company was located in Lynn Realty Trust Company Building #6, located at 278–288 Broad Street at Marshall's Wharf. They shared the building with the George E. Coffin Shoe Company and the P.J. Harney Shoe Company. The above photograph shows a sole leveler in the making room of the Burdett Shoe Company, while the photograph below is of women in the stitching room there. Both pictures were taken in 1919. (Courtesy of the Atlanticare Hospital.)

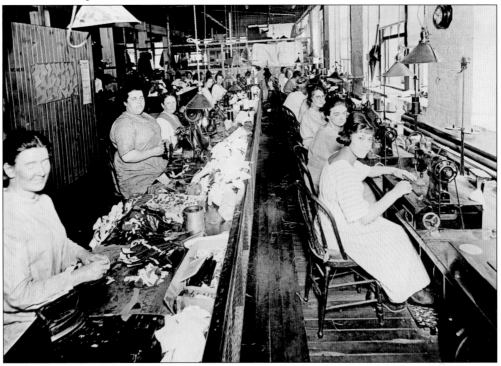

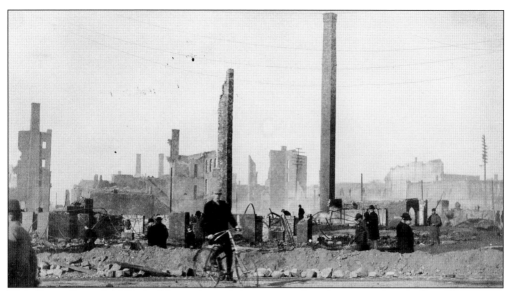

The Great Fire of 1889. In November of that year a fire that started in a glove factory on Almont Street and quickly swept over 31 acres, destroying over 380 buildings in the center of Lynn. Numerous shoe factories, tanneries, banks, newspapers, and a church, as well as 150 residences, were destroyed. (Courtesy of the Peabody Essex Museum, Salem, MA.)

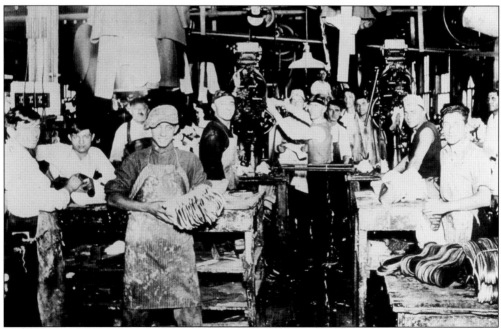

Matzeliger lasting machines can be seen in the background of this 1915 photograph of the lasting room in a Lynn shoe factory. Inventor Jan Matzeliger helped to revolutionize the shoe industry with his invention, originally patented in March 1883. (Courtesy of the Atlanticare Hospital.)

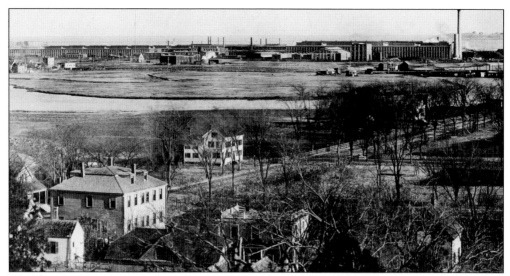

The history of the General Electric Company goes back to April 15, 1892, when Lynn's Thomas-Houston Company merged with the Edison General Electric Company of Schenectady, N.Y. That enterprise grew into one of America's largest corporations and has contributed much to the economy and well-being of the city of Lynn, as well as to many areas of our life in the past and present day. The following pictures are of the Lynn River Works plant. This picture was taken about 1905 from the top of Fox Hill, looking back at the River Works from Ballard Street. (Courtesy of David Carpenter, Lynn General Electric Co.)

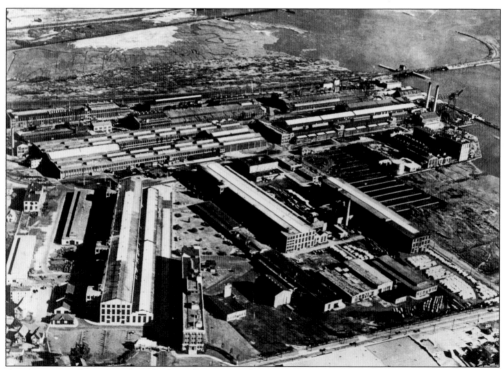

A 1930s aerial view, taken before the Gear Plant Complex was erected. (Courtesy of David Carpenter, Lynn General Electric Co.)

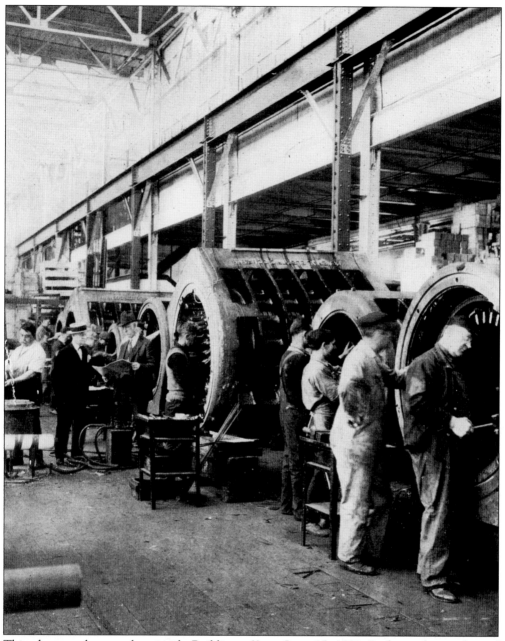

This photograph was taken inside Building #63 on June 15, 1923. It shows the winding of turbine stators in support of the electrical-generating business in Lynn. The man on the far left was said to have begun working for the company in 1889. (Courtesy of David Carpenter, Lynn General Electric Co.)

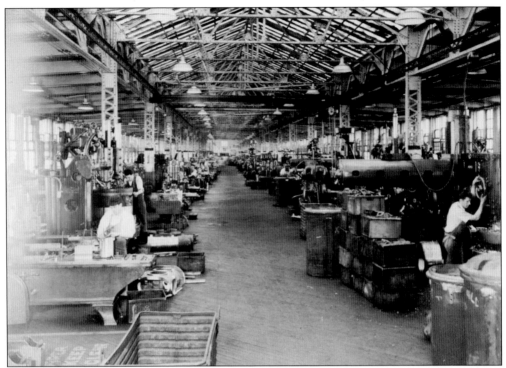

A 1939 view of the apprentice department on the top floor of Building #3-40. (Courtesy of David Carpenter, Lynn General Electric Co.)

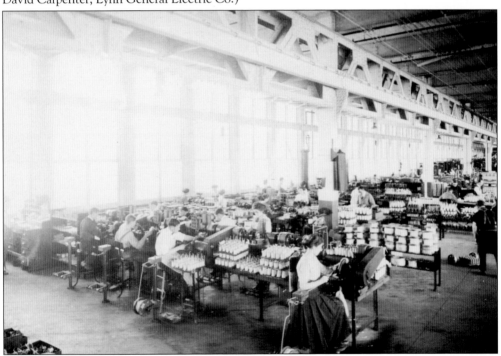

This *c.* 1920 photograph shows workers in the Arc Lamp winding department of Building #2–40. (Courtesy of David Carpenter, Lynn General Electric Co.)

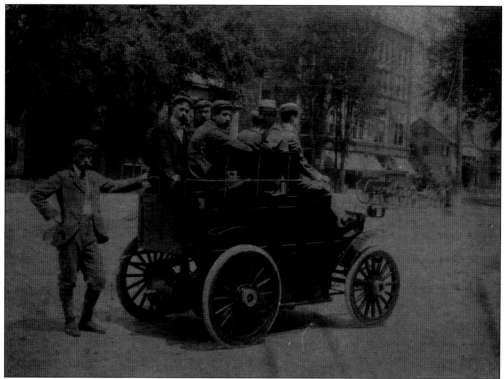

The Thompson Wagonette, a 3 hp, 75-volt car, was built by General Electric in 1897. It is shown here at the south end of Lynn Common. (Courtesy of David Carpenter, Lynn General Electric Co.)

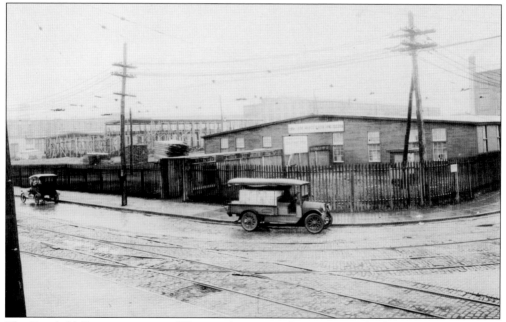

The Fairchild Street entrance at Western Avenue in the 1920s. At the left is Building #45–68 and to the right is Building #77. (Courtesy of David Carpenter, Lynn General Electric Co.)

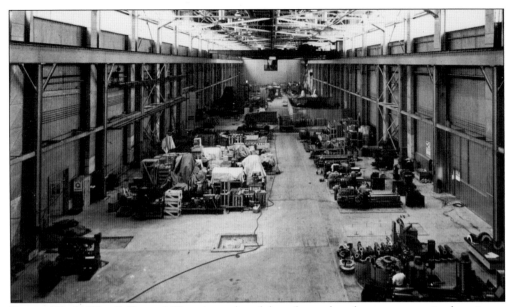

During World War II General Electric workers labored at reduced temperatures in the winters to save on fuel. (Courtesy of David Carpenter, Lynn General Electric Co.)

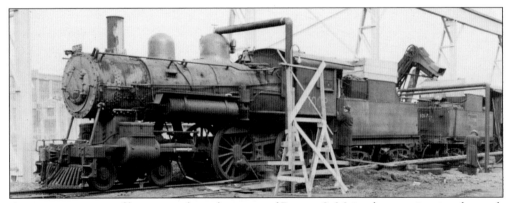

A temporary source of heat came from the steam of Boston & Maine locomotives, so the work on gears could start for the war effort. In the above photograph, taken on April 27, 1941, the interior of a 90-foot gear bay is being heated by one such locomotive. (Courtesy of David Carpenter, Lynn General Electric Co.)

Four

ALONG THE SHORE

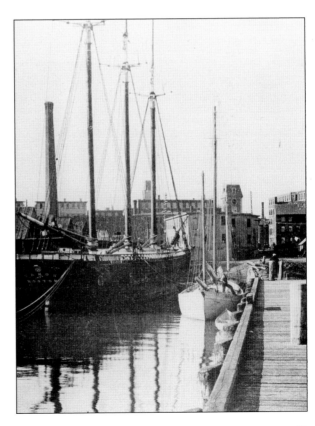

A coal schooner tied up at the wharf, with Lynn's factories in the background. (Photo courtesy of the Lynn, MA Public Library.)

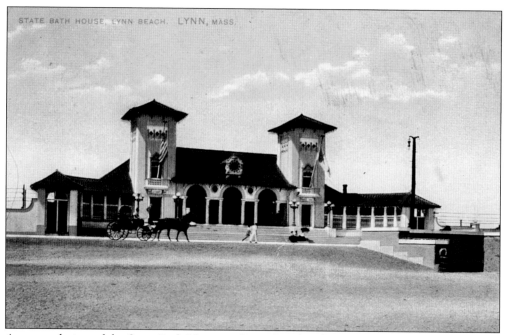

A postcard view of the State Bath House on Lynn Beach, taken in the early 1900s. The State Bath House was a popular place for many years, but was torn down in 1966–67.

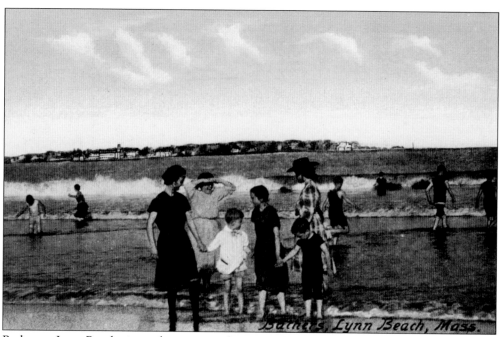

Bathers at Lynn Beach pictured in a postcard view, c. 1915. Note the bathing dress and stockings of the girl in the foreground.

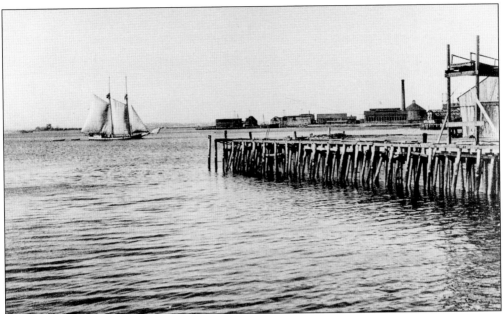

A fishing schooner sails into port. To the right of the photograph is Breed's Wharf, and the Lynn Gas and Electric Company plant can be seen in the background. (Photo courtesy of the Lynn, MA Public Library.)

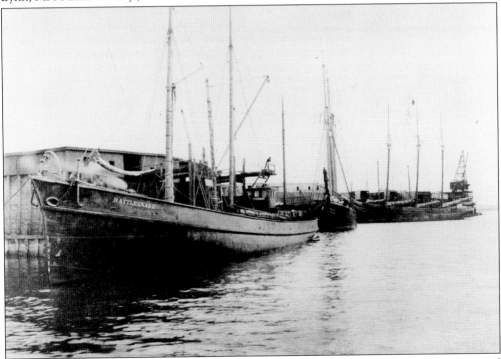

With the coming of coal-burning furnaces, the shipping of coal became a major business, and many coal schooners traveled in and out of Lynn Harbor. Pictured here are the *Rattlesnake* and several other schooners tied up at one of Lynn's wharves. (Photo courtesy of the Lynn, MA Public Library.)

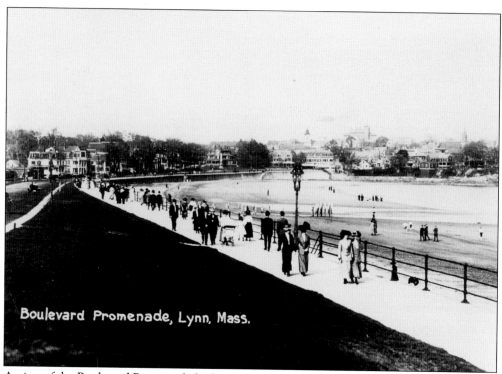

Boulevard Promenade, Lynn, Mass.

A view of the Boulevard Promenade looking toward Swampscott, as people enjoy a stroll along the promenade and the beach as well. (Courtesy of Martha Lewis.)

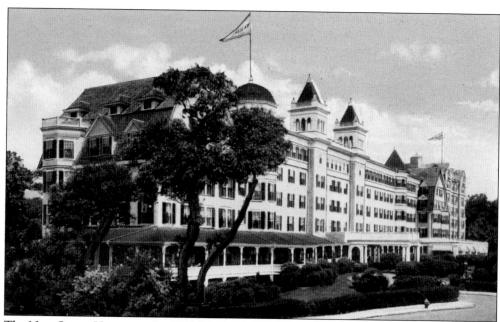

The New Ocean House, on the "Old Puritan Road" in Swampscott, was one of the largest and most successful summer hotels on the North Shore.

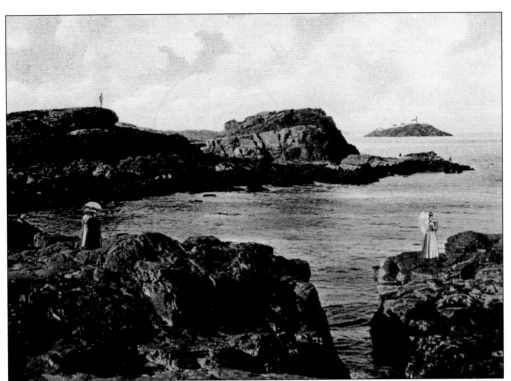

A 1906 postcard view of ladies with their parasols, out on the rocks to get a closer view of the ocean. Castle Rock and Egg Rock can be seen in the distance.

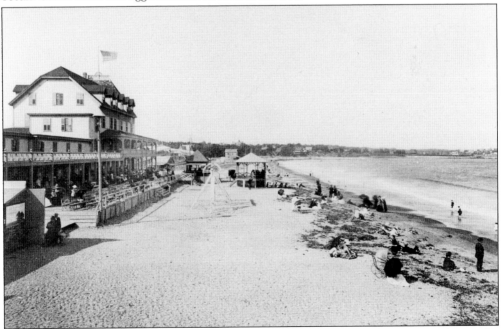

The Nahant Hotel's long piazza was a great place for people to relax in comfort and have the beach and ocean right in front of them. This photograph was taken between 1880 and 1890. (Photo courtesy of the Lynn, MA Public Library.)

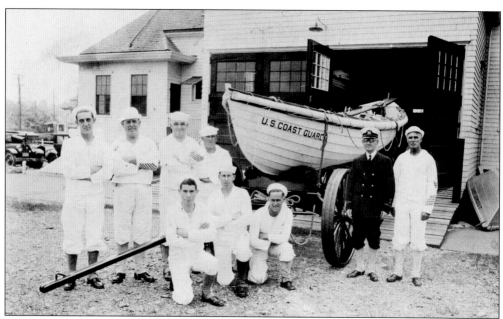

This picture, taken in the first quarter of the century, shows the crew and surf boat of the Nahant Coast Guard Station at the rear of the building. The officer-in-charge is Captain Frank Gove, with Boatswains Mate George Wickens to his left. Edward Ward (standing, second from left) and Charles Jessome (kneeling in the middle) were coastguardsmen who later became Nahanters. (Courtesy of the Nahant Historical Society.)

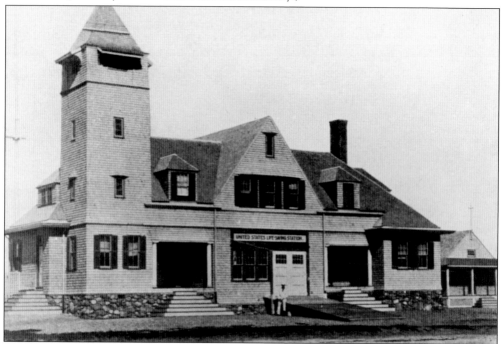

The Nahant Life Saving Station, which opened in 1898, is no longer active in sea rescue work, but is still maintained by the Federal Government as a seasonal recreational facility for members of the armed forces. (Courtesy of the North Shore Jewish Historical Society.)

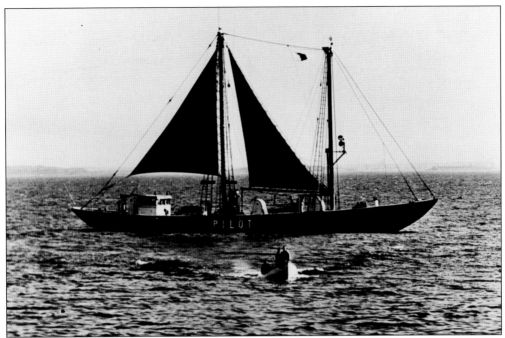

The schooners of the Boston Pilots' Association were a familiar sight in the waters of Nahant Bay for many generations. Several times a week the *Pilot #1* or the *Roseway* would put in to Tudor Wharf to pick up or drop off a pilot. In 1972 motor launches replaced the sail-powered schooners, and the *Pilot #1* was sold, to be used on the West Coast and Hawaii. However, the *Pilot #1* returned in July 1986 to win the celebrated schooner race in Gloucester under the command of Captain John Wigglesworth of that city. (Courtesy of the Nahant Historical Society.)

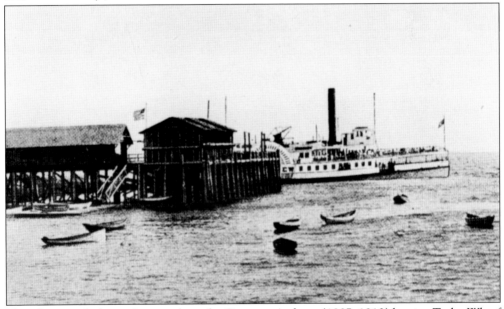

This photograph shows the steamboat the *Governor Andrews* (1907–1910) leaving Tudor Wharf on a return trip to Boston. (Courtesy of the Nahant Historical Society.)

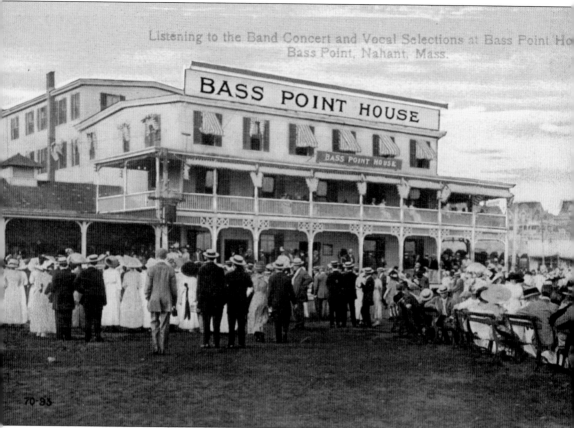

BASS POINT HOUSE

BASS POINT HOUSE

70-93

The Bass Point House, located at Bass Point in Nahant, was a favorite gathering place by the shore. In this picture people have come to listen to the "Band Concert and Vocal Selections." Many of the ladies are dressed in long white dresses and hats, while the most of the men wear straw hats, which were very popular in that era.

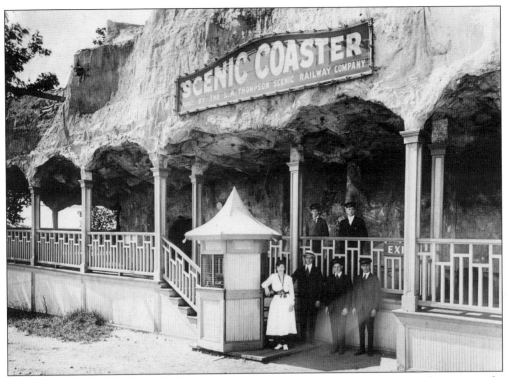

Built by L.A. Thompson in 1911, the Scenic Roller Coaster was a thrilling ride as its tracks skirted the ocean. Some Nahanters may remember the merry-go-round and dancing, which served to add to the excitement as well. Pictured here are, from left to right: (front row) Pearl Kolloch (later Mrs. Frank Lewis), Rollin Southwick, Frank Lewis, and G. Byron Goodell; (back row) Mr. Gauthier and Henry Kolloch, both from management. (Courtesy of the Nahant Historical Society.)

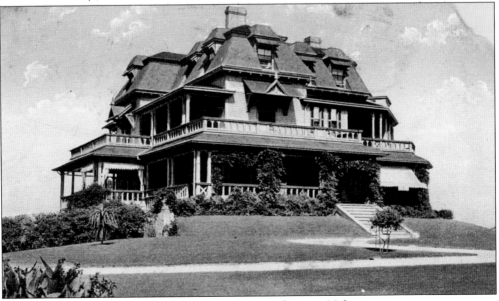

A postcard view of Senator Henry Cabot Lodge's residence in Nahant.

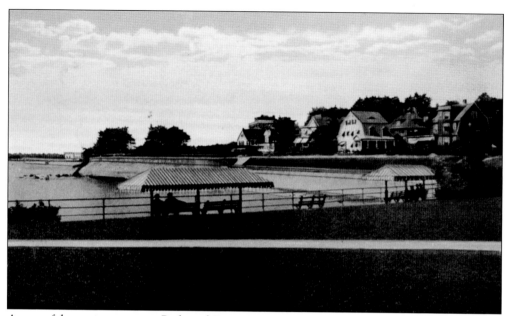

A peaceful evening scene at Park and Deer Cove along Shore Drive in Lynn. This postcard photograph dates from *c*. 1930.

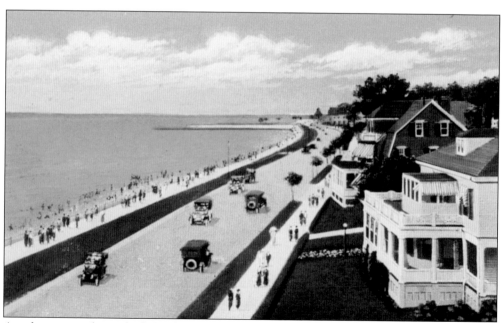

Another postcard view looking along Shore Drive, from Swampscott to Lynn.

Five

CELEBRATIONS
AND PARADES

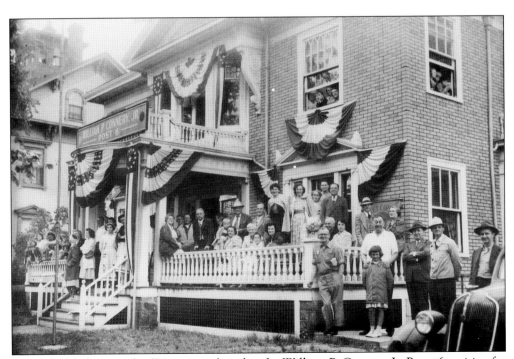

A wonderful photograph of Lynners gathered at the William P. Connery Jr. Post #6, waiting for the 1950 Lynn Centennial Parade to come their way. (Courtesy of Lynn City Hall.)

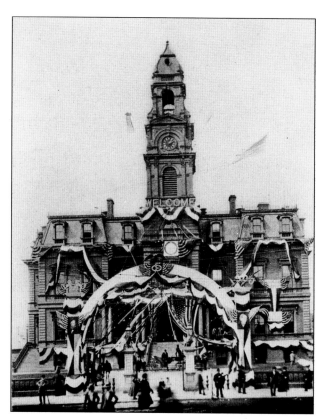

In May 1900 Lynn celebrated its 50th year as a city. Festivities were scheduled for three days, buildings were decorated, parades marched down the streets, and people turned out for a special program at the Lynn Theatre on the eve of the festivities. Lynn City Hall sported its own banners and flags as it sat in readiness for the celebration. (Courtesy of the Newburyport Public Library.)

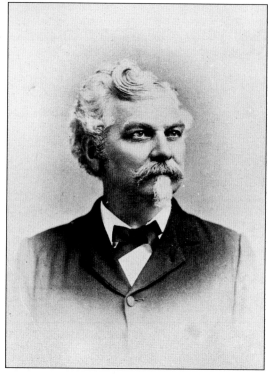

Honorable William Shepherd was mayor of Lynn at that time (1899–1900) and officiated at the ceremonies of the day. (Courtesy of the Newburyport Public Library.)

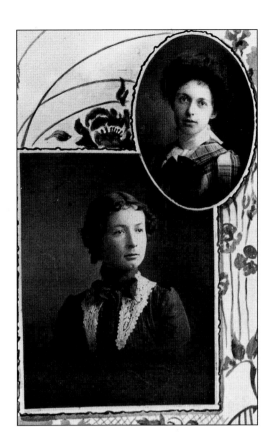

Two young ladies that participated in the exercises were Isabelle Dorothea O'Brien and Mabel Ward. Mabel gave a rendition of the "anniversary poem" in a "pleasing and impressive manner." (Courtesy of the Newburyport Public Library.)

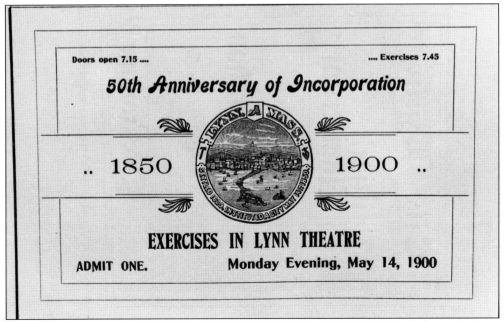

Admission tickets for attendance at the Theatre Exercises were imprinted with the Lynn City Seal. (Courtesy of the Newburyport Public Library.)

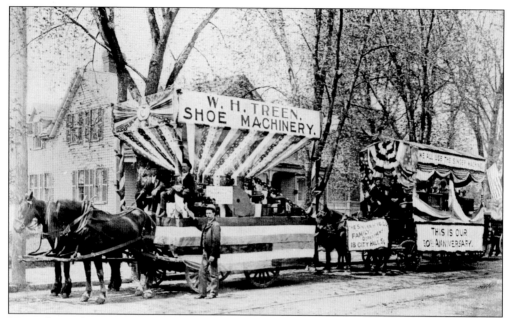

Horse-drawn floats were entered in the trades division of the parade, and featured displays from W.H. Treen Shoe Machinery and the Singer Manufacturing Company family business, located at 18 City Hall Square. (Courtesy of the Newburyport Public Library.)

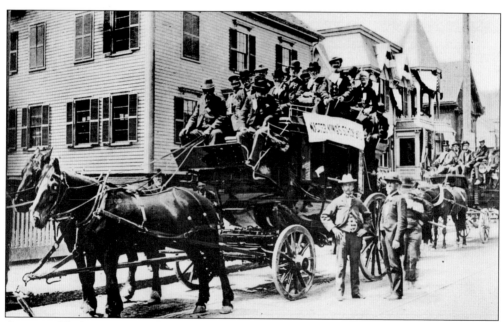

Carriages filled with Master King's school boys wait to start in the parade. Schoolmates Edward S. Newhall and William Stone, directors of their "expedition," are standing in the foreground. (Courtesy of the Newburyport Public Library.)

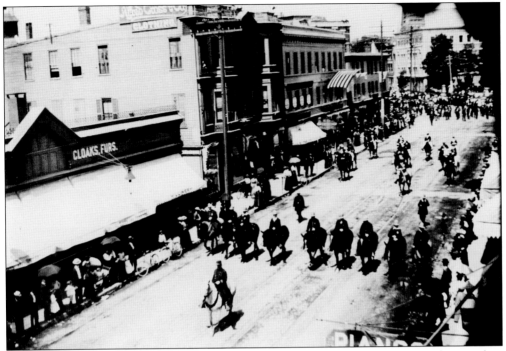

This photograph of Lynn Police on horseback as they ride in a Fourth of July parade was taken from a second-story window in 1879. They are shown coming down Market Street from city hall. (Photo courtesy of the Lynn, MA Public Library.)

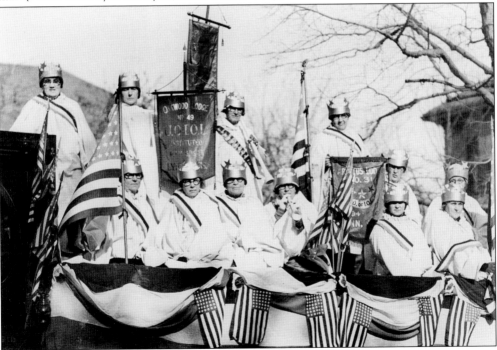

The Odd Ladies Float in the 1928 Armistice Day Parade. (Photo courtesy of the Lynn, MA Public Library.)

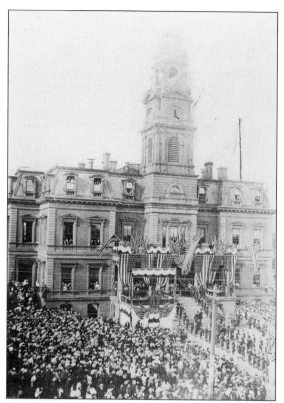

Crowds thronged to see "Teddy" Roosevelt when he visited Lynn in 1902, during a political tour of the area. Here he walks up the steps of city hall with Mayor William Shepherd. (Photo courtesy of the Lynn, MA Public Library.)

President Theodore "Teddy" Roosevelt visited Nahant on August 25, 1902, and is shown here making a speech in front of the Nahant Public Library. To the right is Joseph T. Wilson (the chairman of the Board of Selectmen), as well as other selectmen, Senator Henry Lodge Sr., and the secretary of the navy. In the foreground members of the NDC police stand at attention, while members of the press, in their top hats, busily write up the President's speech. (Courtesy of the Nahant Historical Society.)

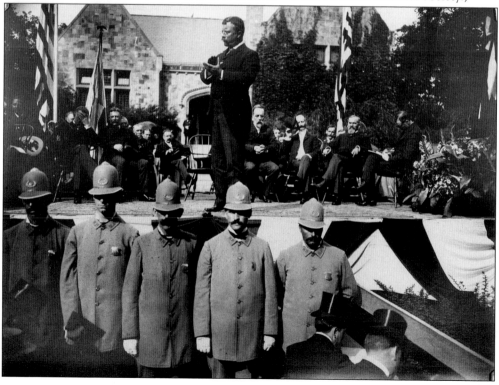

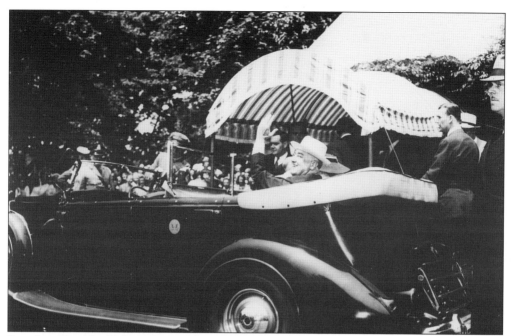

President Franklin Delano Roosevelt and his wife Eleanor are shown arriving in Nahant. The occasion was the marriage of their son John to Anne Lindsey Clark, on June 18, 1938. The reception was held at the Nahant Country Club. (Courtesy of the Nahant Historical Society.)

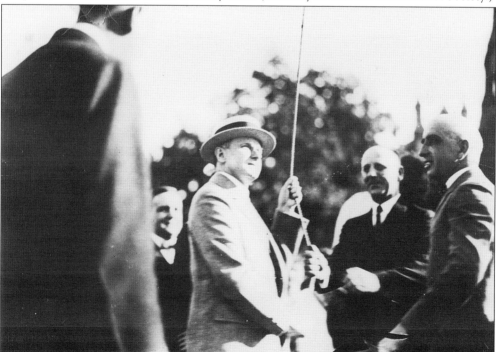

Several visits were made to Lynn in the 1920s by President Calvin Coolidge. He is shown here raising the flag on Lynn Common on August 27, 1925, at the dedication of a new flag pole. (Photo courtesy of the Lynn, MA Public Library.)

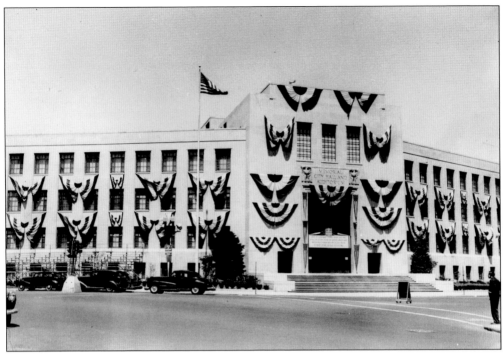

At the 1950 centennial celebration of Lynn's first one hundred years as a city, Lynners once again turned out for two days of festivities. City hall is patriotically draped in readiness for the big celebration. (Courtesy of Lynn City Hall.)

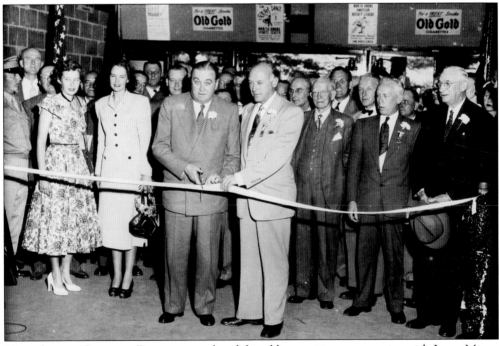

Massachusetts Governor Dever was on hand for ribbon-cutting ceremonies with Lynn Mayor Tarbox and other dignitaries. (Courtesy of Lynn City Hall.)

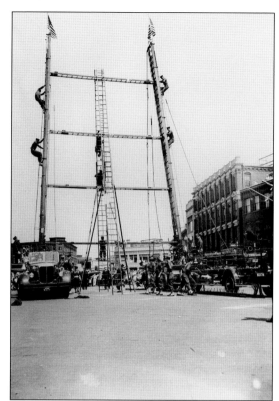

A firemen's muster caught the attention of many as the men climbed to dizzying heights on the ladders to demonstrate their abilities. (Courtesy of Lynn City Hall.)

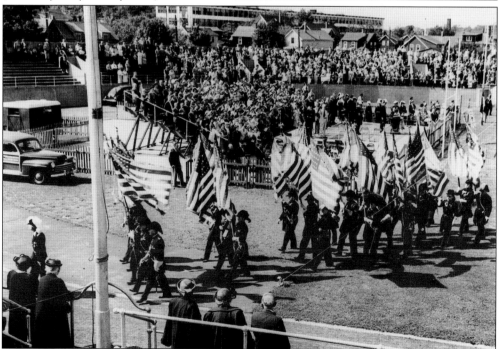

The Knight Templars are shown marching out of Manning Bowl after a ceremony there. (Courtesy of Lynn City Hall.)

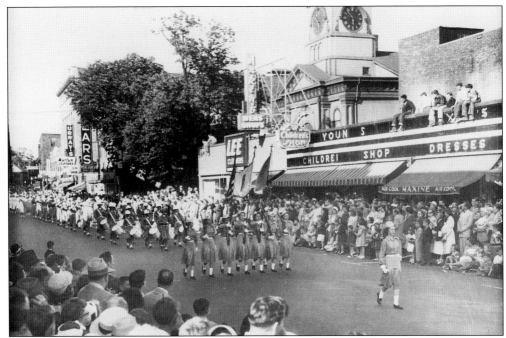

Spectators crowd both sides of the street, and even sit on rooftops, as the Drum and Bugle Corps marches past all the shops. To the left of the photograph, behind the tree, is Sears, Roebuck & Company. (Courtesy of Lynn City Hall.)

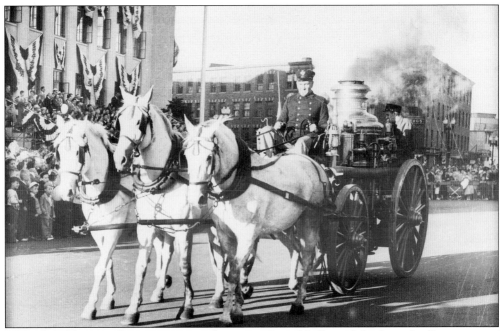

Even the old steam fire engine was taken out of mothballs and fired up for the occasion. (Courtesy of Lynn City Hall.)

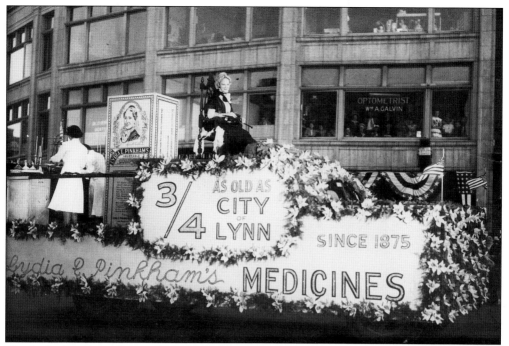

The Lydia Pinkham float included a replica of her laboratory, and reminded people of one of Lynn's "firsts." (Courtesy of Lynn City Hall.)

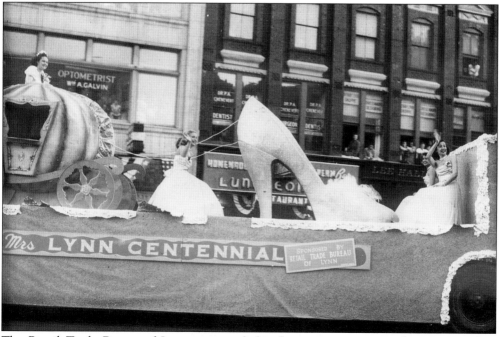

The Retail Trade Bureau of Lynn sponsored this float commemorating the women's shoe industry of Lynn, which was first in the country in production and quality for many years. (Courtesy of Lynn City Hall.)

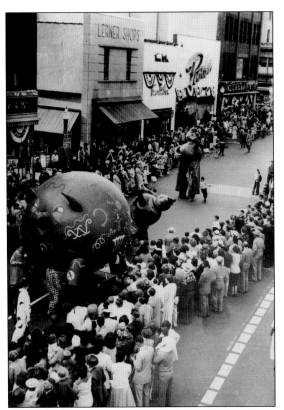

People crowd in closer to get a better look at the inflated pig as it rolls past the Lerner Shops and the Five and Ten. In the right center of the picture a young boy is dwarfed by the size of the clown he is standing next to. (Courtesy of Lynn City Hall.)

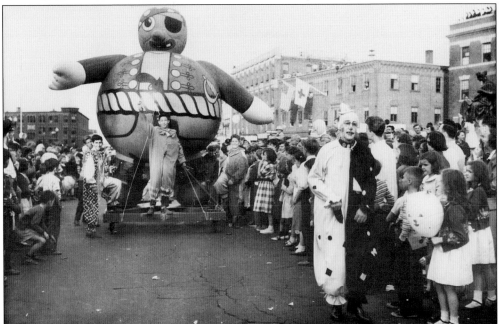

Smiling young clowns accompany the pirate float as it moves down the street; however, the clown in the right of the photograph looks, perhaps, a little worn out. Note the twins to the right of the clown. (Courtesy of Lynn City Hall.)

Six

SCHOOLS

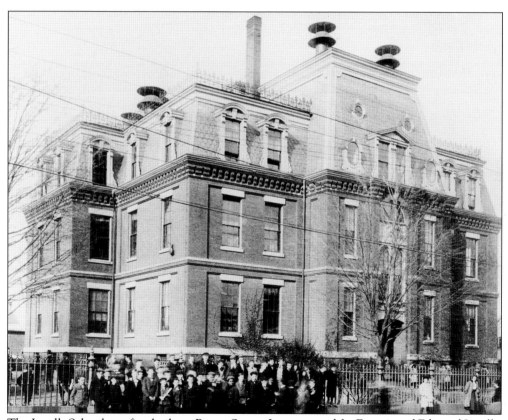

The Ingalls School was first built on Parrot Street. It was named for Francis and Edmund Ingalls, the first settlers of Lynn, and built on the site of their original settlement. It was later rebuilt on Essex Street in 1871. (Photo courtesy of the Lynn, MA Public Library.)

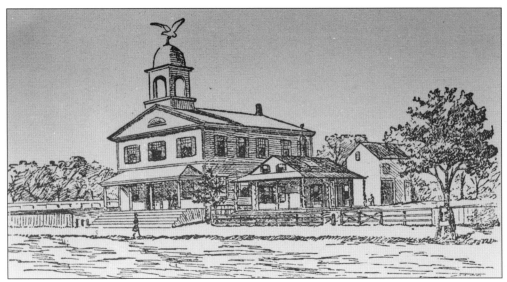

Lynn Academy first opened in April 1805, on South Common, between Vine and Commercial Streets. It cost $3,000 to build and was the first private school for secondary education, remaining in use until 1849. Upon erection of the Lynn High School in 1852, it was sold and moved several times until finally resting at the corner of Centre Street and Western Avenue. In 1905 it became the paint shop of ex-Mayor William L. Baird. (Courtesy of the Mount Carmel Lodge.)

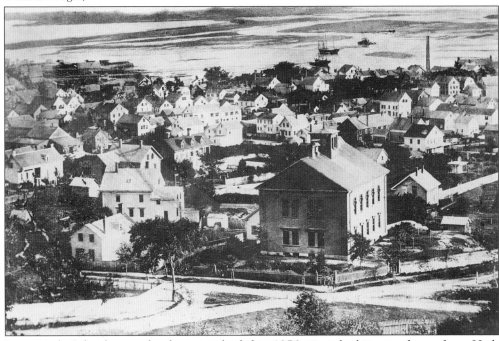

Lynn High School is in the foreground of this 1856 view, looking southeast from High Rock, as the city stretches beyond to the harbor. Due to severe overcrowding, the Lynn Classical and English High School was built in 1892, and the older high school was then converted into a shoe school to train workers going into the shoe industry. (Courtesy of the Atlanticare Hospital.)

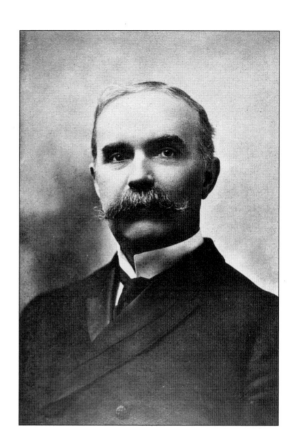

The Lynn Classical and English High School, built in 1892 in Highland Square, looked quite grand with its twin turrets and arched doorways. It was built to house both the English and Classical High Schools.

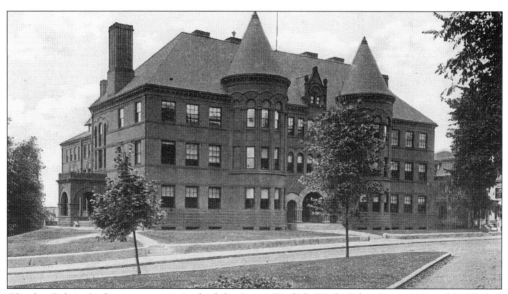

Charles Selvin Jackson was principal of the Lynn English High School in 1915 and held that position for twenty-five years, each year being unanimously re-elected by the school committee. In 1915 Mr. Jackson was also a "graduate" of Lynn English, as he left to assume the duties of superintendent of Lynn Public Schools. (Courtesy of the Lynn English High School.)

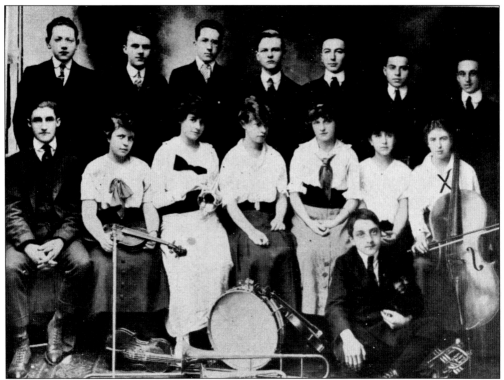

The school orchestra at Lynn English poses for a yearbook picture in 1915. From left to right are: (front row) Akeroyd, Kellam, Morrison, Hitchcock, Webster, Blaisdell, Gardner, and Phillips (sitting); (back row) Sugarman, Hayes, Gordon, Wilcox, Marcus, Edelstein, and Preston. (Courtesy of the Lynn English High School.)

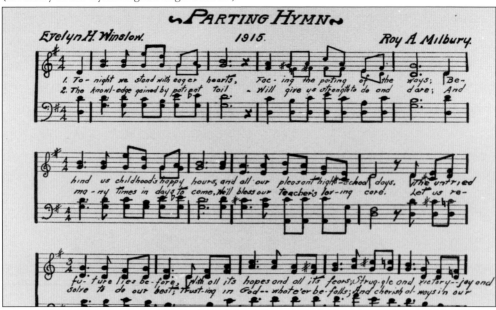

Roy A. Milbury wrote the music, and Evelyn H. Winslow the words, to the seniors' "Parting Hymn" as they graduated in 1915. (Courtesy of the Lynn English High School.)

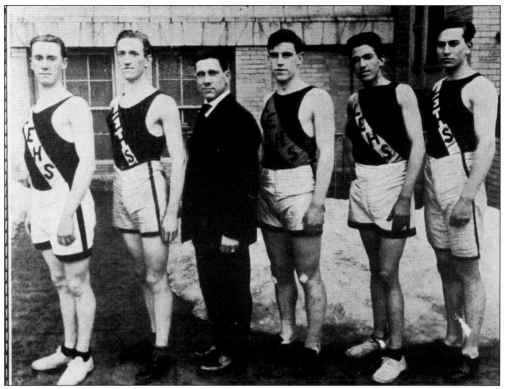

Lynn English had a busy sports program in 1915. The above photograph is of the relay team with their coach; below, the baseball club poses for the school yearbook with coach Boyson. (Courtesy of the Lynn English High School.)

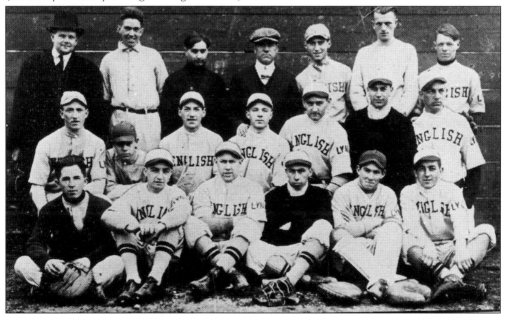

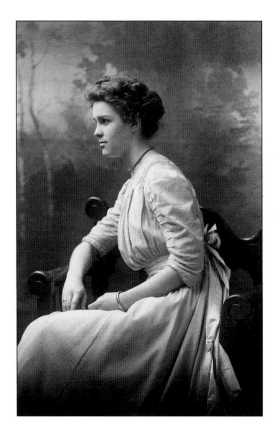

Evelyn C. Richards is pictured in 1910 at the time of her graduation from Lynn English High.

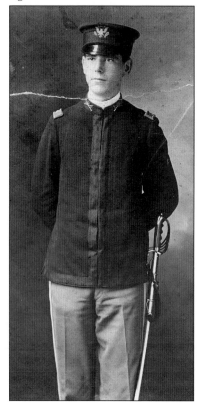

This photograph of Fred T. Phillips, a 1907 graduate of Lynn English, shows him in his uniform of the high school marching battalion.

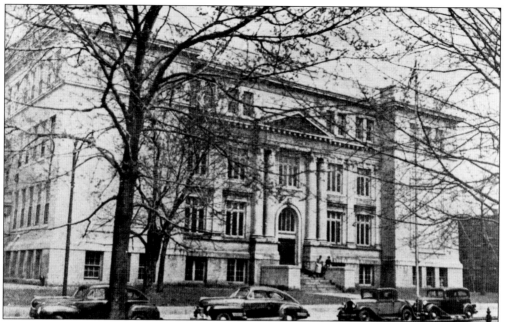

A late 1940s picture of the Lynn Classical High School, with cars parked in front along North Common Street. (Courtesy of the Lynn Classical High School.)

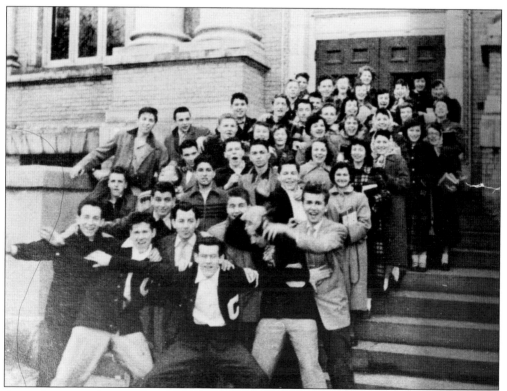

An exuberant graduating class on the front steps of the Classical High School in 1949. (Courtesy of the Lynn Classical High School.)

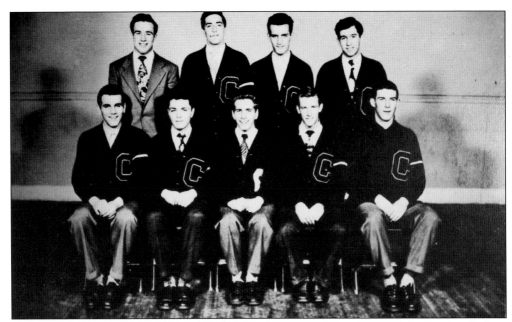

The basketball team of the Classical High School, wearing their team sweaters, pose with their coach for a yearbook picture in 1949. (Courtesy of the Lynn Classical High School.)

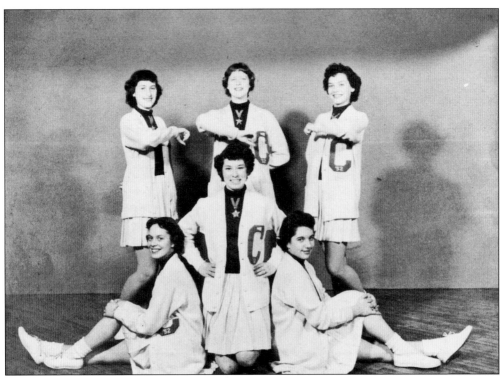

Lynn Classical cheerleaders smile for a yearbook picture the same year. (Courtesy of the Lynn Classical High School.)

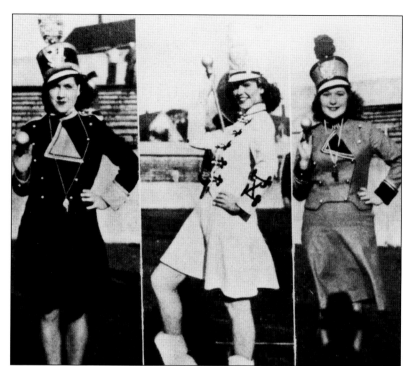

Lynn English majorettes, *c.* 1943. From left to right are Catherine Carozza, Rosemary Cole, and Mary Louise Hannon. (Courtesy of the Lynn English High School.)

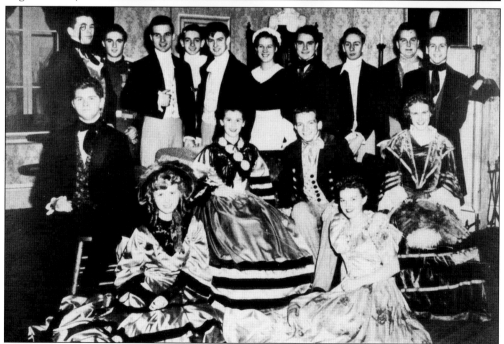

Pictured are members of the Lynn English High School Class of 1949 in their class play. From left to right are: (front row) Betty Paulsen and Jean Kozlowski; (middle row) Eugene Zack, June Quigley, William Rourke, and Muriel Feffen; (back row) James Canning, Robert Ostrer, Richard Guppey, Alan Gruber, Thomas Culliton, Ruth McGinn, Richard Kenerson, Murray Simmons, Fred Spinney, and Richard Chandler. (Courtesy of the Lynn English High School.)

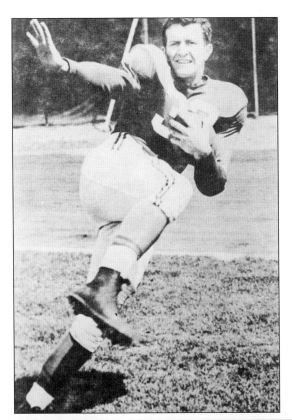

A well-known athlete and sports legend at that time was Harry Agannis, who played for the Classical High School. Lynn Classical and later Boston University retired #33, the number Harry wore throughout his school years. (Courtesy of the St. George Greek Orthodox Church.)

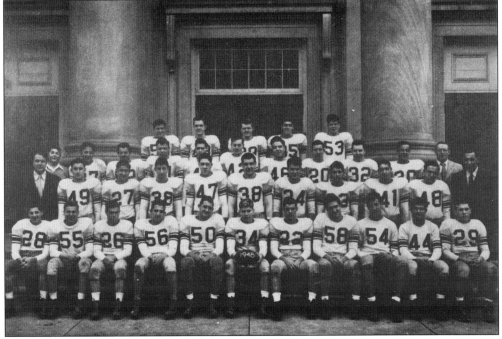

The Lynn English football team and coaches in 1949. (Courtesy of the Lynn English High School.)

80

Seven

Places of Worship

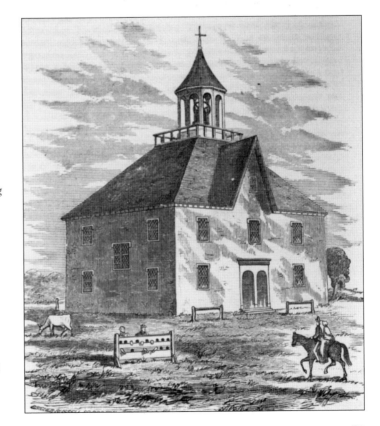

The Old Tunnel Meeting House was built on Lynn Common in 1682, with lumber taken from trees on the Common and from Lynn Woods. It remained in use for over a hundred years, both as a religious meeting place and for public uses as well. After being moved and remodeled, the Old Tunnel Meeting House became the home of the Universalist Church in 1837.

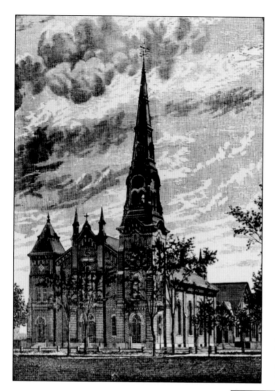

An early illustration of the First Congregational Church located on South Common Street. (Courtesy of the Newburyport Public Library.)

The First Universalist Church was built on Nahant Street in 1873 of brick and stone taken from a rock ledge on Washington Street. An earlier church was built in 1855, but several additions could not contain the congregation, which continued to expand, necessitating the construction of the new church. Sadly, this impressive structure was destroyed by fire in 1976. (Courtesy of the North Shore Jewish Historical Society.)

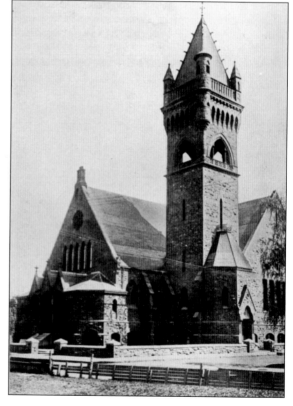

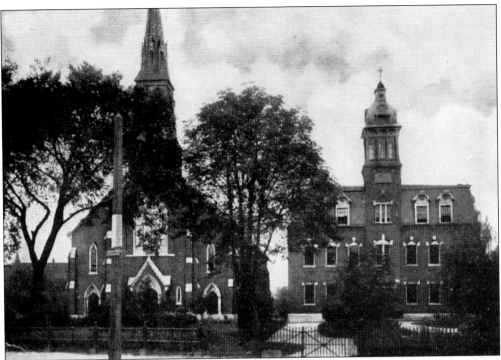

Saint Mary's Church and Parochial School on South Common Street at City Hall Square. The first Catholic church in Lynn, Saint Mary's was dedicated in 1862, after three years of construction. The parish school was opened in 1881, when the Sisters of Notre Dame came to Saint Mary's to act as teachers in the school, and was in existence until 1941, when it was destroyed by fire. (Courtesy of Brother Arcadius, CFX, St. John's Prep, Danvers, MA.)

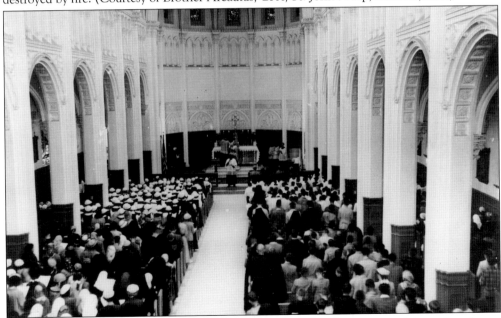

The interior of Saint Pious Church in 1950, as people gather for mass to celebrate Lynn's one hundred years as a city. (Courtesy of Lynn City Hall.)

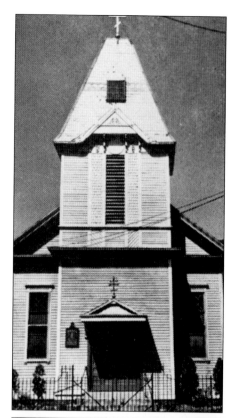

The St. George Greek Orthodox Church was located on Pleasant Street from 1905 to 1913 in a building that, prior to that, had been used as the Swedish Evangelical Church. The first Greek school was established there in 1911, but the congregation steadily grew and space soon became a problem, necessitating the purchase of the church on the Common in 1913. (Courtesy of the St. George Greek Orthodox Church.)

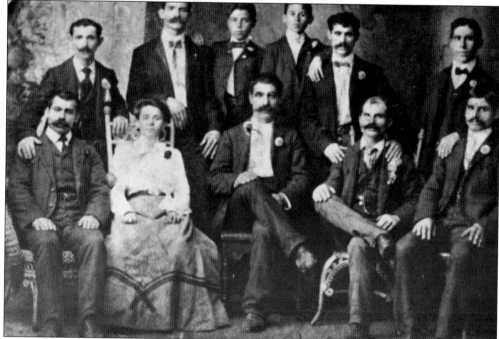

A c. 1900 photograph of one of the early Greek families of Lynn. (Courtesy of the St. George Greek Orthodox Church.)

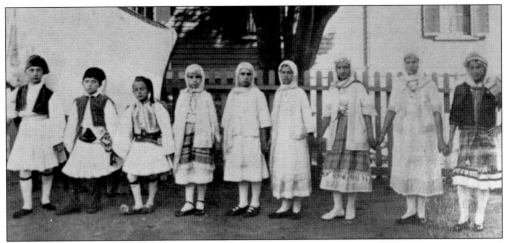

The St. George Class of 1914 pose in their native costume. (Courtesy of the St. George Greek Orthodox Church.)

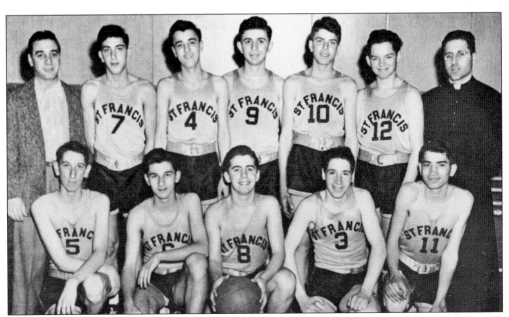

The St. Francis basketball team of 1954. From left to right are: (front row) Ed King, Bob Raptel, captain Bob Serino, Frank Giacoia, and Harry Mancinci; (back row) coach Archie Serino, Bob Cormier, Tom Tortolini, Pat Lussiano, Mike Mancini, Dave Serino, and Reverend Carmen T. Russo.

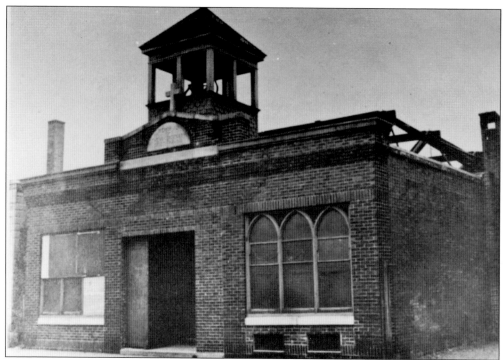

The St. Francis Church. On January 10, 1925, a brick building at 106-108 Blossom Street, formerly a mattress factory, was bought by the church, and the first services were held on Easter Sunday of that year. It was later destroyed by fire on September 8, 1954. (Courtesy of Brother Arcadius, CFX, St. John's Prep, Danvers, MA.)

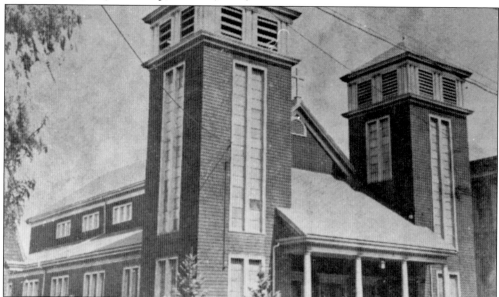

A view of St. Michael's Church and Parochial School, which served Lynn's Polish community. St. Michael's Archangel R.C. Church, at the corner of Summer and Cottage Streets, was dedicated on April 24, 1906. (Courtesy of Brother Arcadius, CFX, St. John's Prep, Danvers, MA.)

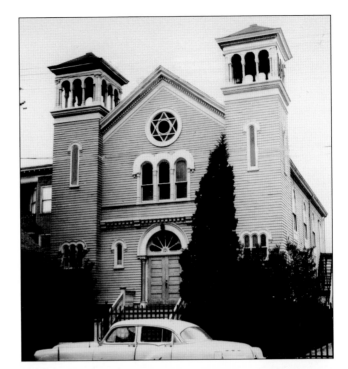

Built in 1900 at 151 Ocean Street, the Ahabat Shalom was the first Jewish synagogue on the North Shore. This photograph was taken in the 1950s. (Courtesy of the North Shore Jewish Historical Society.)

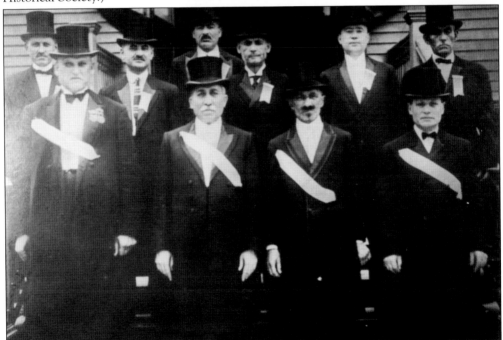

The Anshai Sfard was located at the corner of Commercial Street and South Common. Standing on the steps in the picture below are the founding members of the Anshai Sfard in 1919. From left to right are: (front row) Max Taitsman, Samuel Levine, David Freemerman, and the treasurer (name unknown); (back row) Saul Chalek, Mr. Hymanson, and Sam Galis (second from the right). (Courtesy of the North Shore Jewish Historical Society.)

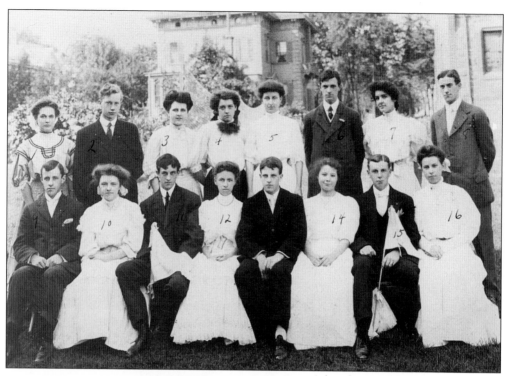

A handsome young group of Saint Stephens Associates posing on the church lawn. The organization was formed in 1906, but disbanded only four years later in 1910. (Courtesy of the St. Stephens Episcopal Church.)

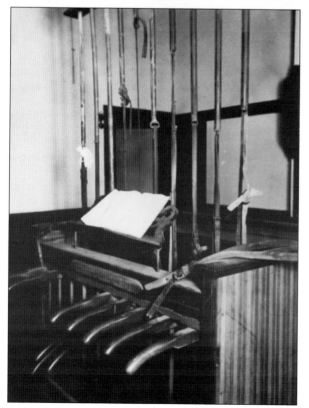

The tower chimes of St. Stephens, cast in England, are as old as the church itself, and were celebrated in Longfellows poem *The Bells of Lynn*. They were originally played from a keyboard under the tower (shown here), but after many years of use the chimes had to be restored (1961), and were then played from a small console near the organ. (Courtesy of the St. Stephens Episcopal Church.)

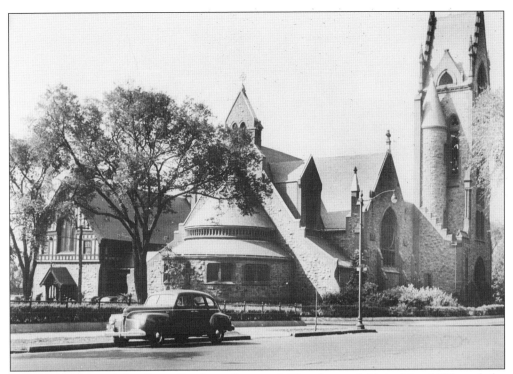

The cornerstone of the Saint Stephens Episcopal Church was laid in May 1881, and the church was consecrated that November. The church's donor, Honorable Enoch R. Mudge, died suddenly before the consecration, and at his request he and other members of his family were buried in the churchyard. (Courtesy of the St. Stephens Episcopal Church.)

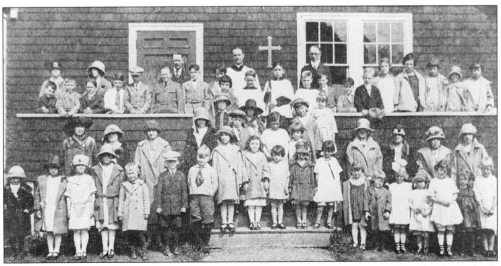

St. Stephens expanded with missions in both East and West Lynn, and schools in both locations. This is a picture of the first school at West Lynn, taken about 1926. (Courtesy of the St. Stephens Episcopal Church.)

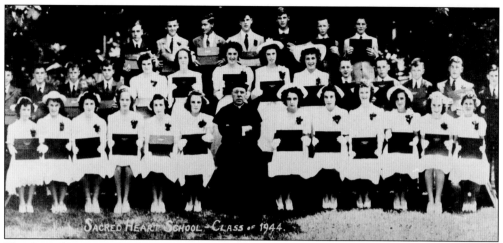

The Sacred Heart School Class of 1944 hold their diplomas as they pose for a picture with Father Sallaway. (Courtesy of Brother Arcadius, CFX, St. John's Prep, Danvers, MA.)

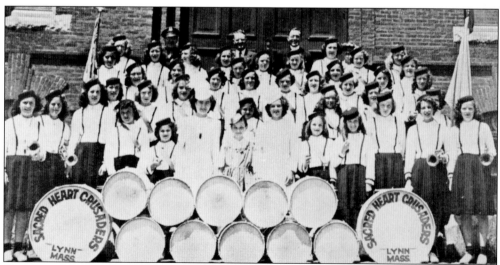

The Sacred Heart Crusaders musical marching outfit was the first girls' marching outfit in the parish and were prominent in local and area competitions. The drum and trumpet corps was organized in 1942, and was made up of girls of grammar school age. (Courtesy of Brother Arcadius, CFX, St. John's Prep, Danvers, MA.)

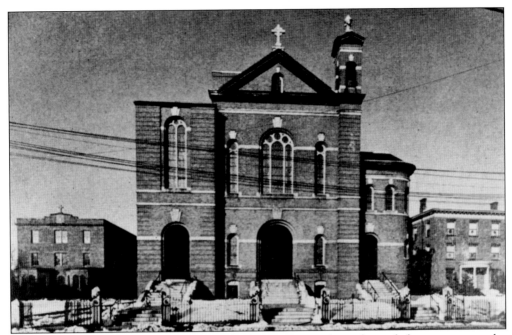

A view of the Sacred Heart Church with the rectory to the right and the convent to the left. Although the parish was established June 21, 1894, masses were celebrated for two years in a cigar factory building on Wyman Street until the present church on Boston Street was completed. (Courtesy of Brother Arcadius, CFX, St. John's Prep, Danvers, MA.)

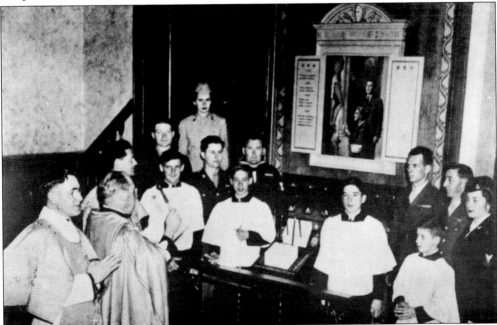

May 30, 1945 was chosen as the date to dedicate the Serviceman's Memorial and Sacred Heart Parish Honor Roll in the lower church. Joining Father Sallaway, pastor, in the blessing and dedication are Father Mullin, Father Sullivan, altar boys, and servicemen and women. (Courtesy of Brother Arcadius, CFX, St. John's Prep, Danvers, MA.)

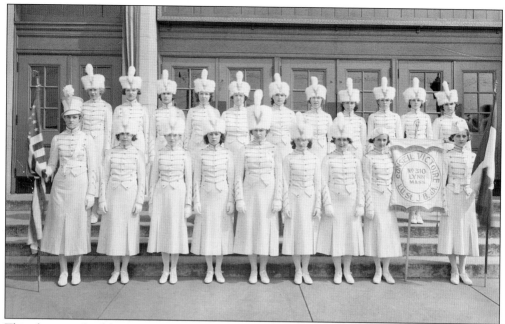

This photograph of the Conseil Victoire #310 of St. Jean's Church was taken at the Premire Prix parade in Providence, Rhode Island, on September 7, 1936. The captain is Rita L'esperance; holding the banners are Mary Barrows and Irene Michaud; and the flag bearer is Rita Jenkins.

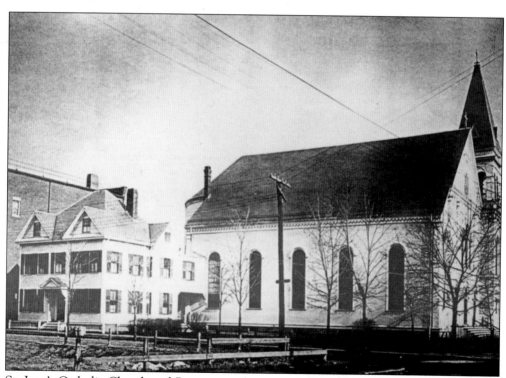

St. Jean's Catholic Church and Rectory, at the corner of Franklin and Endicott Streets, was built to serve the growing French population of Lynn. This photograph was taken in 1910.

Eight

SERVICES AND ORGANIZATIONS

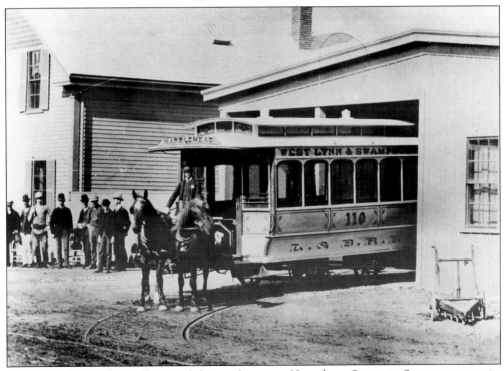

A horse-drawn trolley pulls out of the car barns on Humphrey Street in Swampscott on its way to Marblehead in 1884. The advent of the first electric trolley was four years later. (Photo courtesy of the Lynn, MA Public Library.)

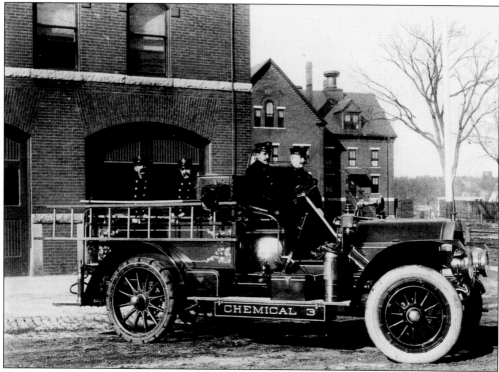

Firemen sit on Chemical #3 in front of the Tower Hall Station on Boston Street. One of the first pieces of motor-driven fire apparatus used by the Lynn Fire Department, Chemical #3 was in use by 1914. (Photo courtesy of the Lynn, MA Public Library.)

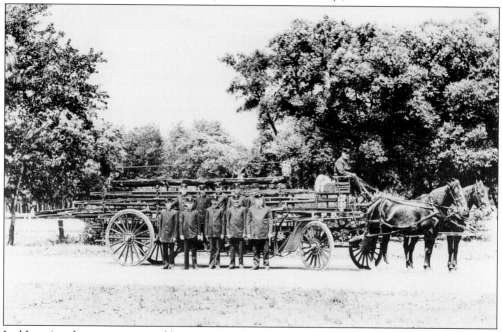

Ladder #4 and crew are pictured here in 1906, before the advent of the motor-driven fire trucks. (Photo courtesy of the Lynn, MA Public Library.)

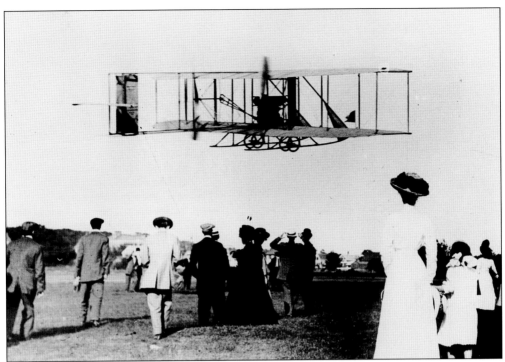

A crowd gathered to watch Harry Atwood as he flew the first air mail delivery in New England from Saugus to Lynn on May 30, 1912. (Photo courtesy of the Lynn, MA Public Library.)

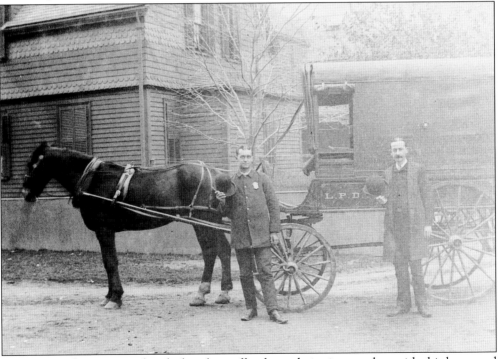

Two Lynn policemen stand with their hats off to have their picture taken with this horse and patrol wagon at 98 Park Street. (Photo courtesy of the Lynn, MA Public Library.)

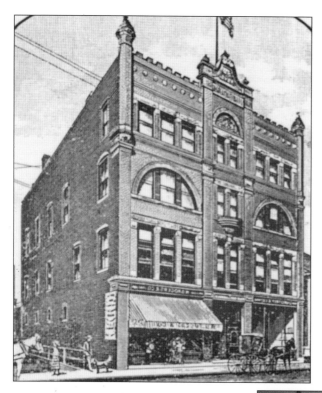

An early illustration of the Grand Army of the Republic Building at 58 Andrew Street. Built in 1885 by the General Lander Post #5, it was the center for many and varied activities throughout the city. The Meeting Hall of Civil War veterans is located on the third floor and has been maintained in its original condition, its walls covered with over 1,200 photographs of the General Lander Post 45 Civil War veterans. Post #5 was considered to be the country's largest in 1885; today it is one of thirteen remaining in the country, and the only one in Massachusetts. (Courtesy of Robert Mathias, Lynn GAR.)

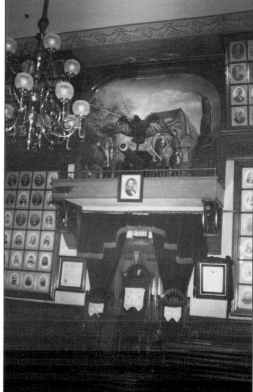

A view of the commander's chair in the Meeting Hall shows some of the pictures of the veterans. (Courtesy of Robert Mathias, Lynn GAR.)

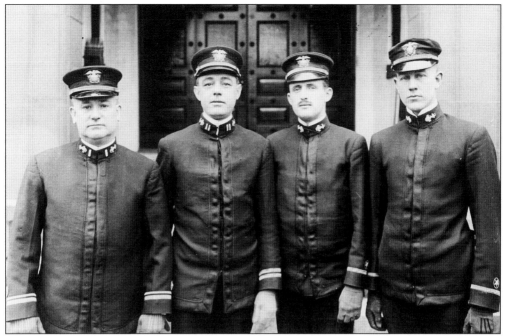

Officers of the U.S.S. *Kearsage* on April 2, 1917, in front of the Lynn Armory. From left to right are Lieutenant E.D. Abbott, Lieutenant Walter G. Howard, Ensign R.P. Hodsdon, and Ensign Harold C. Speed. (Photo courtesy of the Lynn, MA Public Library.)

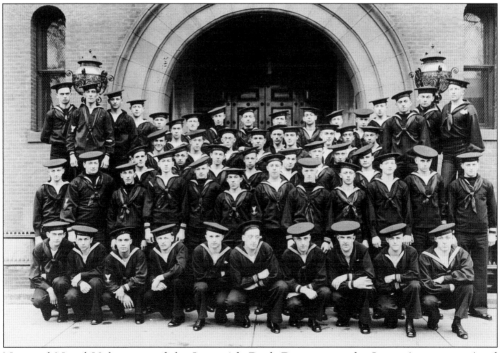

National Naval Volunteers of the Lynn 4th Deck Division, at the Lynn Armory on April 1, 1917, just before leaving for the U.S.S. *Kearsage*. (Photo courtesy of the Lynn, MA Public Library.)

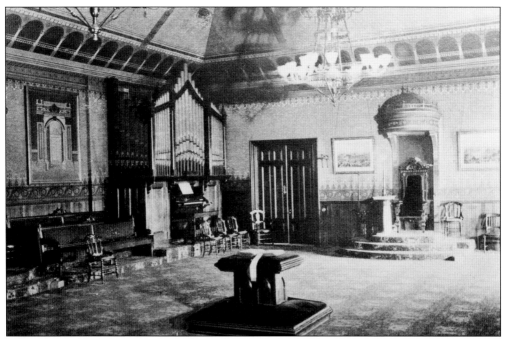

The Mount Carmel Lodge was first organized in 1805 and held its first meetings in the old Lynn Academy. Lodge members later met in a number of other buildings throughout the city until coming to the YMCA Building at the corner of Market and Liberty Streets. Shown here is the Lodge Room as it appeared in 1898 with a large pipe organ in the corner. (Courtesy of the Mount Carmel Lodge.)

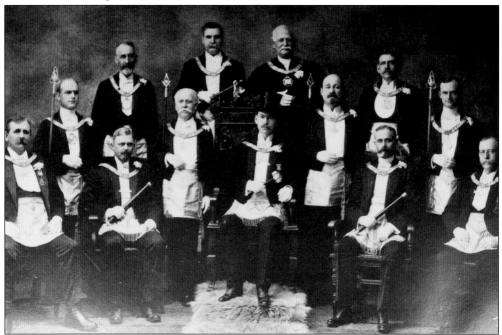

The officers of the Mount Carmel Lodge at their 100th anniversary in 1905. (Courtesy of the Mount Carmel Lodge.)

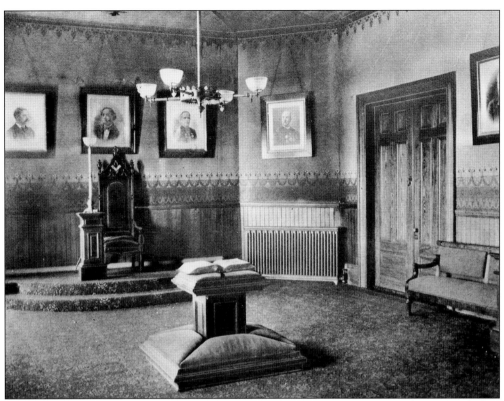

A view of east of Prelate Hall. (Courtesy of the Mount Carmel Lodge.)

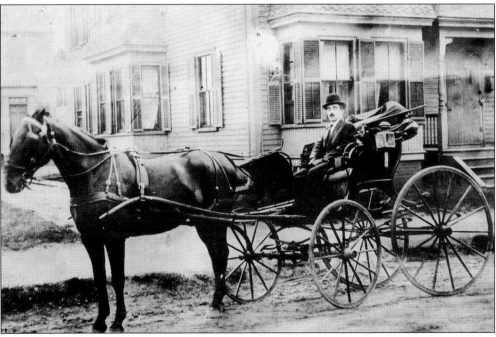

Dr. Leiberman, the first Jewish doctor in Lynn, making house calls in his horse and carriage. (Courtesy of the North Shore Jewish Historical Society.)

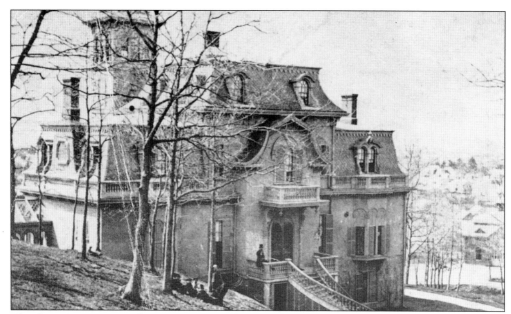

The first Union Hospital opened in the old Tapley Mansion on Linwood Street in September 1901. The mansion was built about 1860 by wealthy leather manufacturer Phillip P. Tapley, and was located at the foot of Wade's Rock, now better known as Lover's Leap. It was a grand place, with an elaborate mahogany staircase, marble floors, and lighting from chandeliers and overhead gas jets. (Courtesy of the Atlanticare Hospital.)

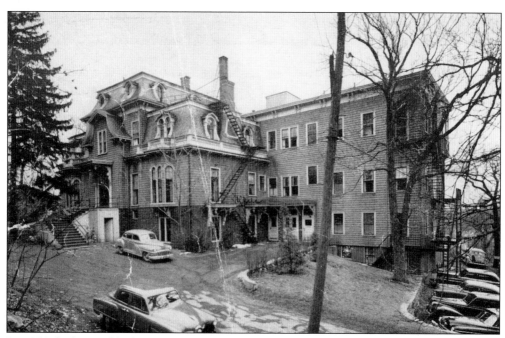

By 1950 the hospital had outgrown the building, despite its large addition, and was increasingly pressed for space. Soon after that a building fund was started and finally in 1953 a new hospital was completed on Lynnfield Street. (Courtesy of the Atlanticare Hospital.)

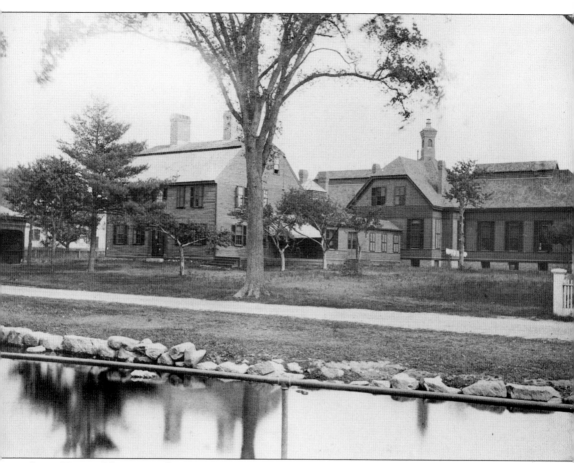

Lynn Hospital first opened in 1883 in the old Hawthorne Mansion on Boston Street. It had ten rooms and one hundred patients were seen there that year. The need for a local hospital arose as a result of the increase in the number of injuries at the local shoe factories. With the advent of more sophisticated machinery to increase shoe production, there also came a greater chance for workers to be injured. Injured workers who could be treated and released were taken to the basement of city hall where they were seen, but workers who were more seriously injured were transported by stretcher to the railroad station platform. Here they waited, often up to several hours, for the next train to Boston. This photograph shows Lynn Hospital at that time, with Strawberry Brook in the foreground. Today, Strawberry Brook runs underground in the same place in front of Lynn Hospital. (Courtesy of the Atlanticare Hospital.)

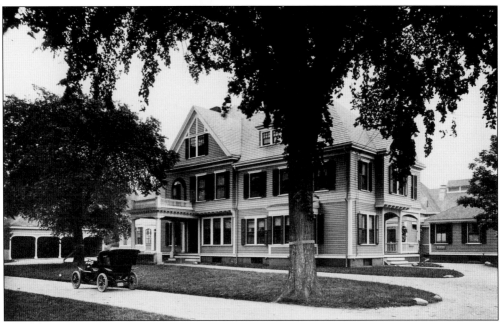

The Lynn Hospital Administration Building opened in February 1892, taking the place of the old Hawthorne House. This photograph was taken about 1910. (Courtesy of the Atlanticare Hospital.)

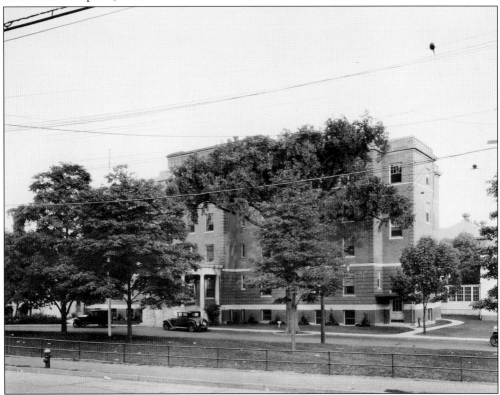

The new Lynn Hospital. (Courtesy of the Atlanticare Hospital.)

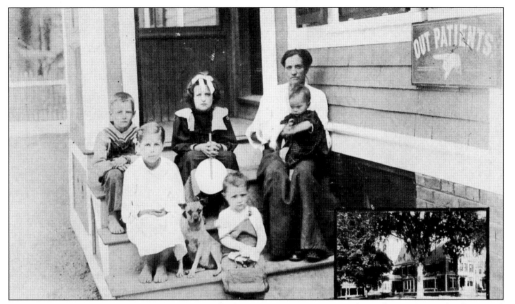

This picture is one of a series of postcards showing various areas of care/services at the hospital just after the turn of the century. In this view, a family waits for services. Note the family dog waiting patiently as well. (Courtesy of the Atlanticare Hospital.)

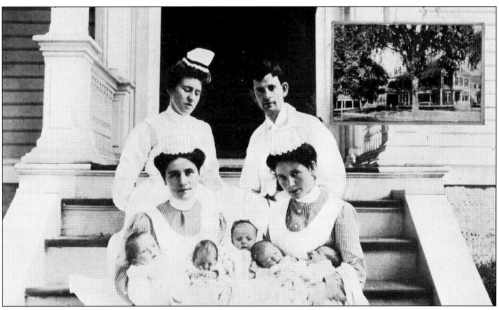

Another postcard view, this time of nurses with five newborns on the steps of the hospital. (Courtesy of the Atlanticare Hospital.)

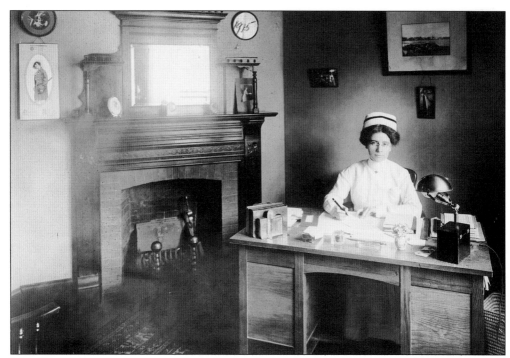

Miss Wyman was the superintendent of nurses and the matron of maternity nurses in 1915. At that time, nurses still wore handkerchief caps. (Courtesy of the Atlanticare Hospital.)

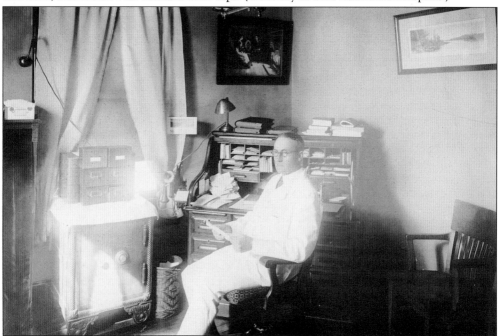

Samuel G. Underhill, M.D., the second resident superintendent of Lynn Hospital, served in that role from May 1, 1914, to September 9, 1918. He was followed by Dr. Simons in March 1919 for a year, and then Miss Allen, from 1920 to 1937. (Courtesy of the Atlanticare Hospital.)

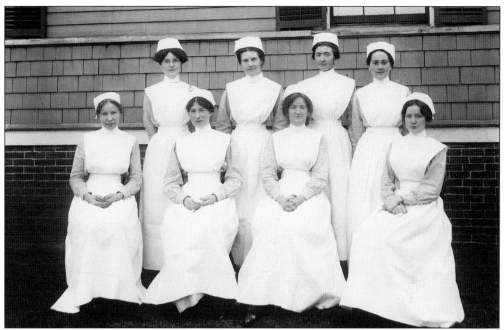

A group of nurses posing for a picture outside Lynn Hospital. From left to right are: (sitting) Alice Churchill, Georgie Alward, Annie Warren, and Emma Ducharme; (standing) Julia Donovan, Annie Mccafferty, Martha Gard, and Flossie Keith. (Courtesy of the Atlanticare Hospital.)

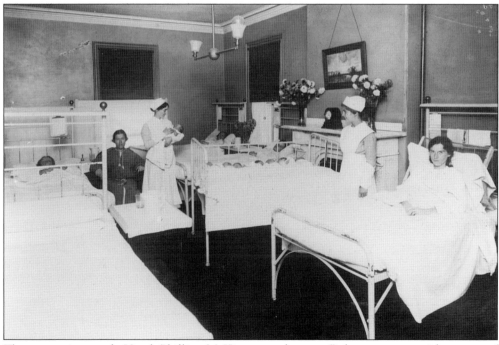

The maternity ward. Hazel Phillips McKinney and nurse Robertson pose with a row of babies all neatly wrapped for their first picture on September 12, 1917. (Courtesy of the Atlanticare Hospital.)

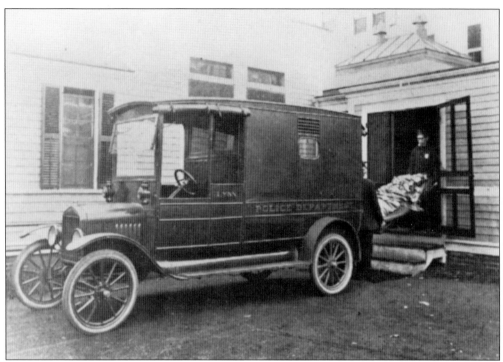

The Lynn Police Department ambulance is backed up to the emergency entrance at Lynn Hospital delivering a patient. (Courtesy of the Atlanticare Hospital.)

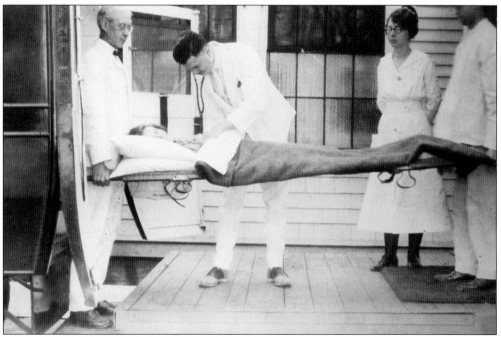

Attendants hold the stretcher as a doctor examines a patient who has just arrived by ambulance at the emergency entrance of the hospital. (Courtesy of the Atlanticare Hospital.)

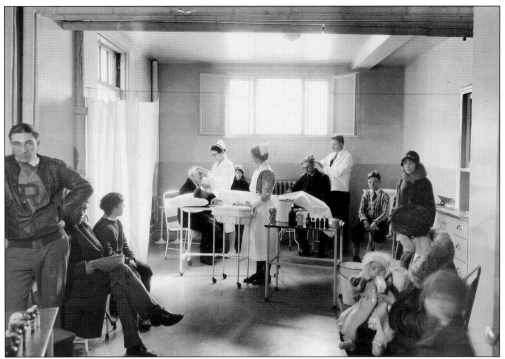

A *c*. 1920 photograph of the busy surgical clinic. (Courtesy of the Atlanticare Hospital.)

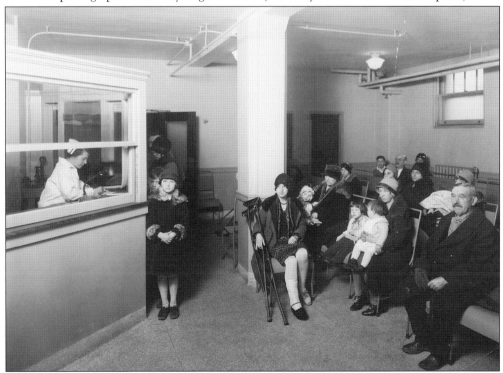

A nurse checks in a patient, as people in the emergency waiting room seem resigned to waiting and sit with their coats on. (Courtesy of the Atlanticare Hospital.)

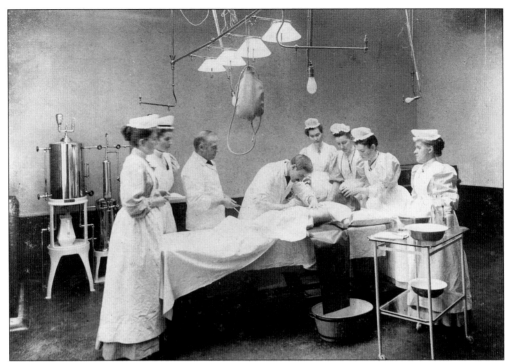

Note the absence of masks and gowns, as well as the less than adequate lighting system, in this 1901 view of the operating room at Lynn Hospital. (Courtesy of the Atlanticare Hospital.)

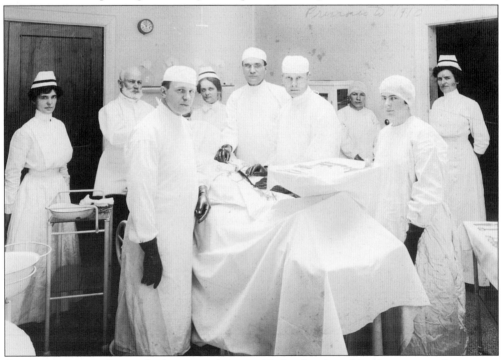

Operating room technique had improved noticeably by the time this picture was taken, seven to eight years later, of the same operating room. (Courtesy of the Atlanticare Hospital.)

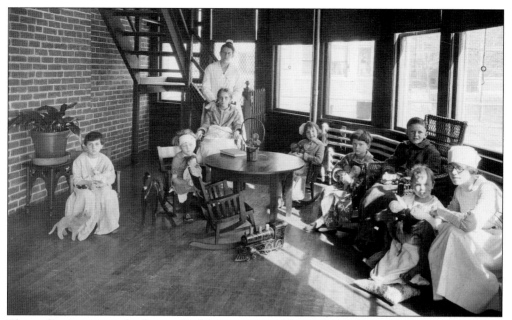

The pediatric unit in the Pevear Building is pictured here about 1920. While recovering from their illnesses, children played with toys that have become popular with collectors today. (Courtesy of the Atlanticare Hospital.)

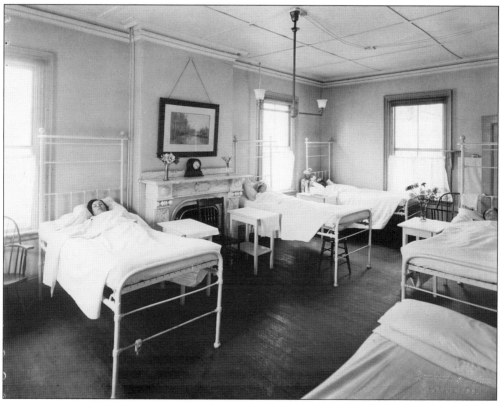

A c. 1917 view of the women's ward at Lynn Hospital. (Courtesy of the Atlanticare Hospital.)

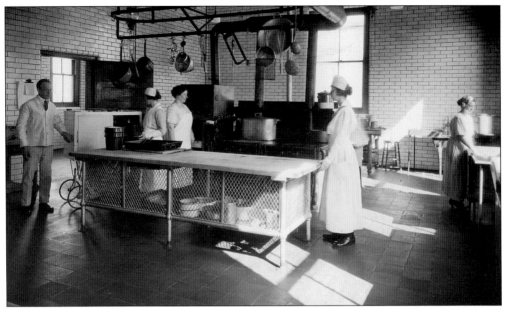

This photograph of the spacious kitchen at Lynn Hospital in 1915 shows the neat functional area where the patients' meals were prepared. (Courtesy of the Atlanticare Hospital.)

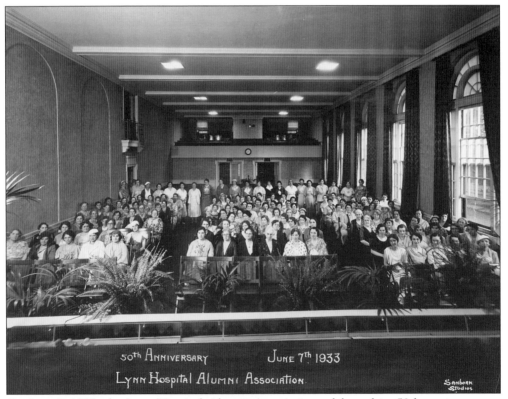

50th ANNIVERSARY   JUNE 7th 1933
Lynn Hospital Alumni Association.

Sanborn Studios

On June 7, 1933, the Lynn Hospital Alumni Association celebrated its 50th anniversary at Ryan Hall. (Courtesy of the Atlanticare Hospital.)

Nine

THE FACES OF LYNN

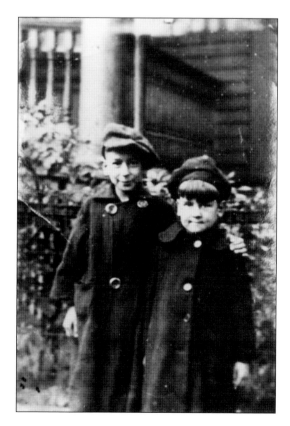

Brothers George (right) and Arthur Zorian pose for a picture outside their home in the Highlands in 1924. George was seven years old at the time this picture was taken. (Courtesy of Janice Zorian Bacon.)

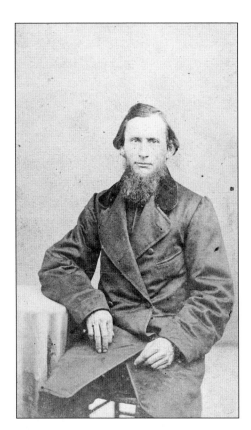

Two early photographs, taken about the time of the Civil War by William T. Bowers, a well-known Market Street photographer in Lynn in the later part of the 1800s. Although they are perhaps father and daughter, they proved impossible to positively identify.

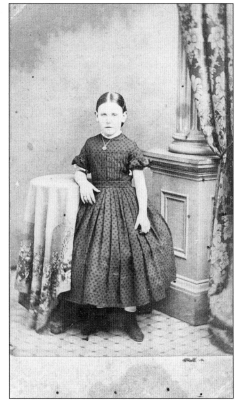

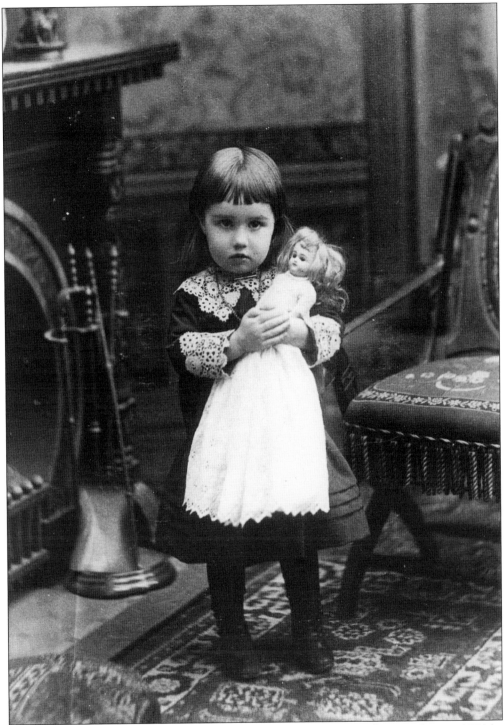

A charming picture of a little girl holding her doll. This photograph was taken in 1886 by Taggard, a photographer whose business was located in the Stevens Building at Central Square. (Photo courtesy of the Lynn, MA Public Library.)

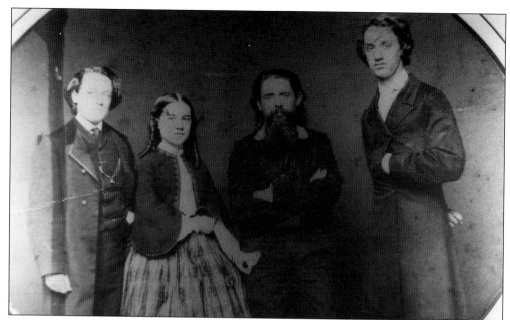

The Hutchinson family, a famous family of singers, made their home at High Rock for many years. They became a popular singing group in the 1840s and traveled all over the world performing their songs. They are credited with much of the work of popularizing the Anti-Slavery movement with their soul-stirring songs and choruses. During the Civil War President Lincoln requested them to sing before the soldiers in various camps, and he himself, on many occasions, listened to their songs with "the greatest of appreciation." Shown here are, from left to right, Judson, Abby, John, and Asa Hutchinson, in a *c.* 1845 photograph. (Courtesy of the Milford, NH Historical Society.)

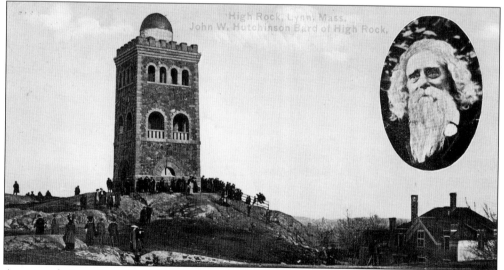

A postcard view of people visiting the High Rock Tower. To the right can be seen part of the Stone Cottage, built by Jesse Hutchinson about 1845. The High Rock Tower was built years later in 1905 at the request of John Hutchinson when he sold the land to the city. The insert is of John Hutchinson, a familiar face about town at that time, with his long white hair and flowing beard.

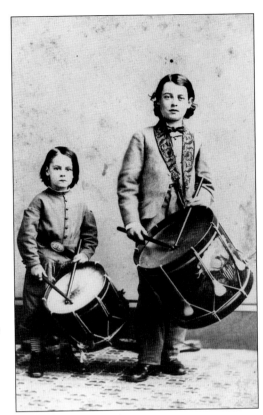

The Hutchinsons, who came from a family of sixteen children, were born in Milford, New Hampshire. They were all accomplished musicians and often had their picture taken with their musical instruments. (Courtesy of the Milford, NH Historical Society.)

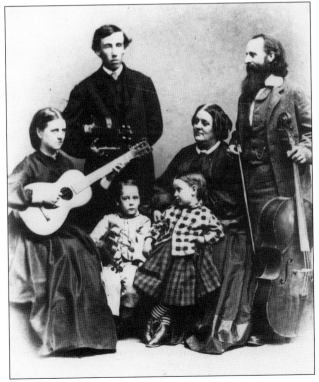

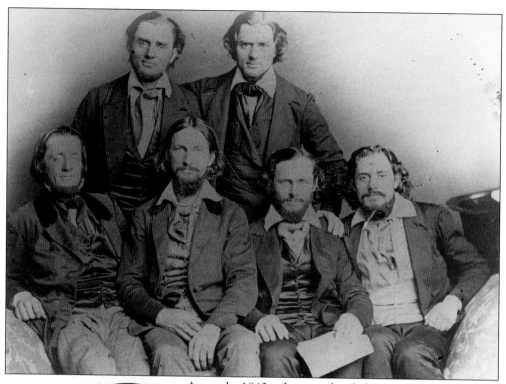

An early 1840s photograph of the Hutchinson brothers. From left to right are: (front) Jessie, Judson, Asa, and John; (back) twins Joshua and Caleb. This photograph was taken by W. Marshall Wires. (Courtesy of the Milford, NH Historical Society.)

Frederick Douglass was an ex-slave who became one of the most influential black Americans in the nineteenth century. Soon after coming to New England in 1838, Douglass so impressed people with an anti-slavery speech he gave that he was hired as a lecturer for the Massachusetts Anti-Slavery Society and became a famous abolitionist and orator. Douglass lived in Lynn from 1841 to 1845, and it was during this period that he wrote his most important work, a narrative of his life as a slave, which later became a background source for Harriet Beecher Stowe's classic anti-slavery novel *Uncle Tom's Cabin*. While in Lynn he became friends with the Hutchinson family, who often accompanied him on his speaking tours, singing patriotic songs as part of the program. (Courtesy of Brother Arcadius, CFX, St. John's Prep, Danvers, MA.)

Alonzo Lewis, the self-styled "Bard of Lynn," was a man of many talents. He was by profession a surveyor, but was also a schoolteacher, poet, and historian, and is perhaps best known for his *History of Lynn*, which contains illustrations and poems by Lewis himself. During the 1840s Lewis became greatly affected by the speeches of William Lloyd Garrison, and was responsible for starting the Anti-Slavery Society in Lynn. (Photo courtesy of the Lynn, MA Public Library.)

A meeting at the camp of Benjamin Johnson in Lynn Woods. From left to right are: (front row) Nathan Hawkes, Charles J.H. Woodbury, William S. Burrill, and Howard M. Newhall; (middle row) J.C. Houghton, C.H. Newhall, Luther S. Johnson, H.F. Tapley, Benjamin F. Spinney, J.L. Parker, and Wilbur F. Newhall; (back row) Phillip A. Chase, Benjamin N. Johnson, Joseph Smith?, and Lewis P. Bartlett?. (Photo courtesy of the Lynn, MA Public Library.)

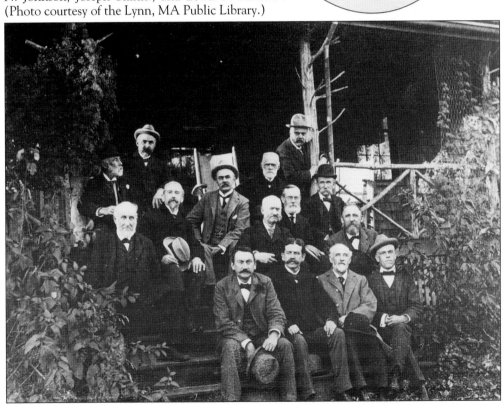

Moll Pitcher was a famous clairvoyant who was reputed to tell fortunes with such amazing accuracy that ship masters often consulted her before setting sail, hoping to gain information about profitable cargoes. She lived at the foot of High Rock after her marriage in 1760 to Robert, a shoemaker, and helped supplement the family income by telling fortunes. Her grandfather, John Dimond of Marblehead, was considered a wizard by some, and was noted for his "ability" to bring ships safely into port during the roughest of gales. (Photo courtesy of the Lynn, MA Public Library.)

This is Hiram Marble standing at the entrance to Dungeon Rock holding a lantern. Hiram Marble came to Lynn in 1851 after hearing of the pirate's treasure reportedly buried at Dungeon Rock. He purchased Dungeon Rock and the land around it, hoping to prove the truth of Spiritualism by finding the treasure with the help of mediums. Hiram, with his son Edwin, began excavating at a cave, work which they would continue for the rest of their lives, but to no avail. (Photo courtesy of the Lynn, MA Public Library.)

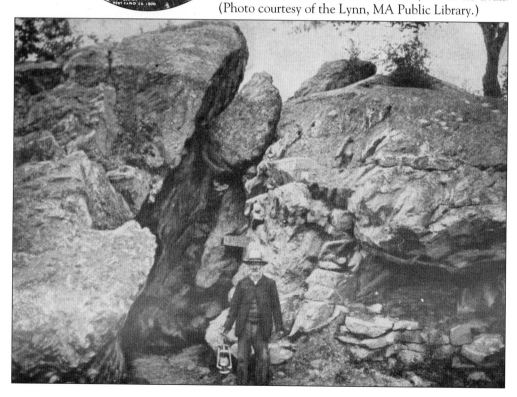

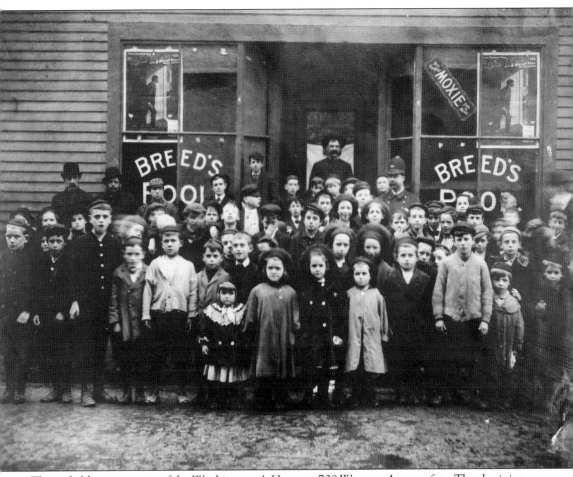

These children are guests of the Workingmen's Home at 709 Western Avenue for a Thanksgiving dinner in November 1908. (Courtesy of the Peabody Essex Museum, Salem, MA.)

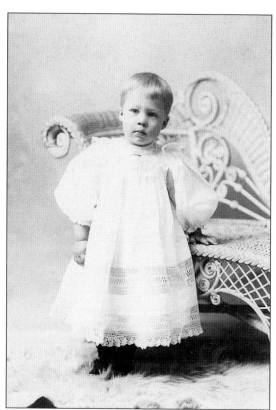

These *c.* 1890s photographs of members of the Eli B. Gloyd family were taken by different photographers. Eli B. Gloyd was in the shoe business with Charles E. Harwood, who later became mayor of Lynn in 1894–95. Note the fancy little dress with puffed sleeves and the scrolled rattan couch behind.

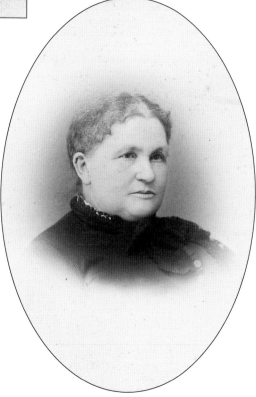

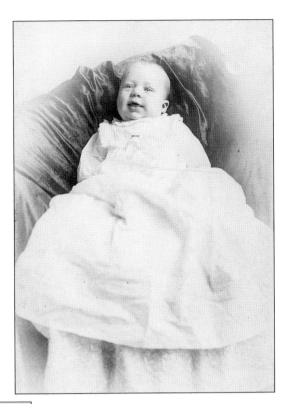

A happy baby, also a member of the
Gloyd family.

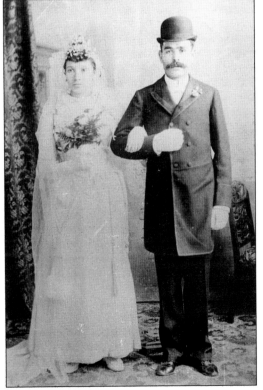

Mr. and Mrs. Simon Samuels, a Jewish
couple on their wedding day. They were
friends of the Margolskee family. This
photograph was taken in the 1890s.
(Courtesy of the North Shore Jewish
Historical Society.)

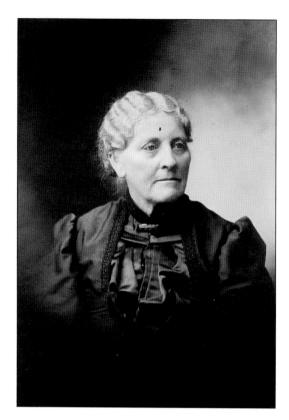

Mrs. Carolus M. Cobb (Bessie Brown), in a photograph taken by W. Marshall Wires when his studio was at 139 Broad Street. Mrs. Cobb was the wife of Dr. Carolus M. Cobb, who wrote *A History of Lynn Hospital*, published in 1918.

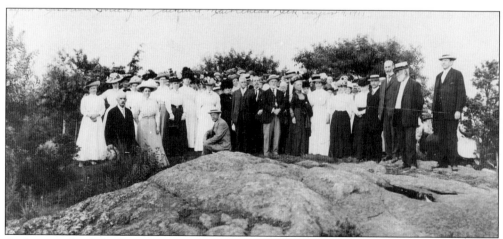

A photograph of the Lynn Historical Society gathered for an outing at Parkhill, Marblehead Neck, on August 9, 1911. (Photo courtesy of the Lynn, MA Public Library.)

122

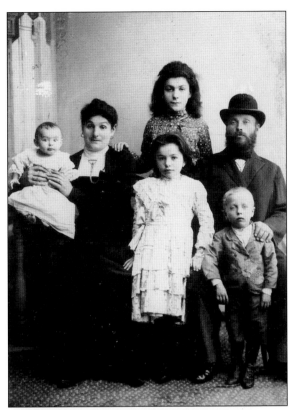

A *c.* 1905 photograph of an immigrant Lithuanian family. Hiram and Rose Freedman pose with their children, Ann, Eve, Bess, and Alex. (Courtesy of the North Shore Jewish Historical Society.)

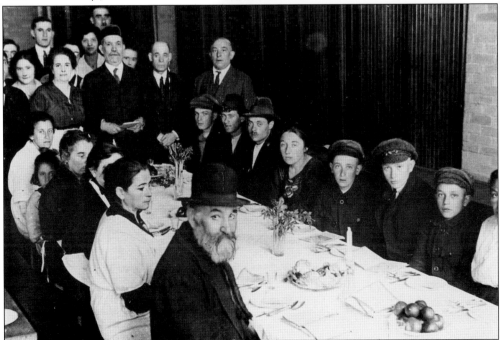

A group of Jewish immigrants gathering for Seder. (Courtesy of the North Shore Jewish Historical Society.)

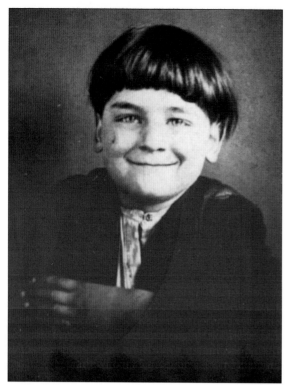

George Zorian has an engaging smile as he poses for his first grade picture in 1924. (Courtesy of Janice Zorian Bacon.)

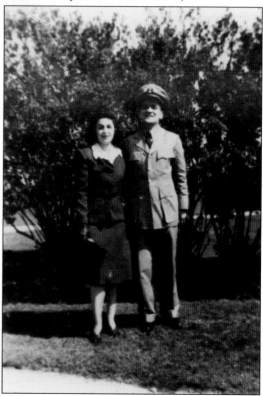

This picture of Mary Zorian and her brother George (in his Navy uniform) was taken in 1942 during World War II. (Courtesy of Janice Zorian Bacon.)

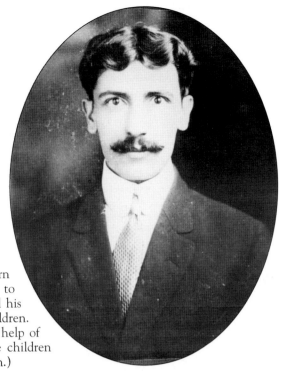

Their father, Phillip Zorian, was born in Armenia about 1890 and emigrated to this country in the early 1900s. He and his wife, Dorothy Surmenian, had four children. She died in 1923 and Phillip, with the help of his mother-in-law, was left to raise the children himself. (Courtesy of Janice Zorian Bacon.)

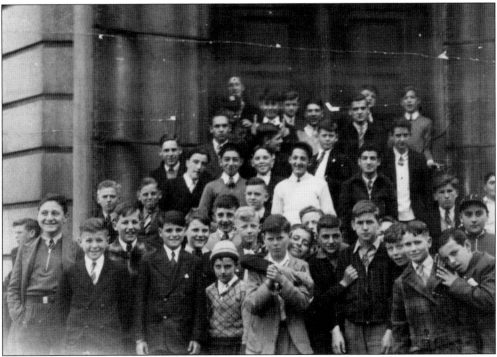

This group of smiling young fellows are all paper boys. They are standing on the steps of the *Lynn Item* Building as the *Item* honored its paperboys, *c.* 1934. (Courtesy of Janice Zorian Bacon.)

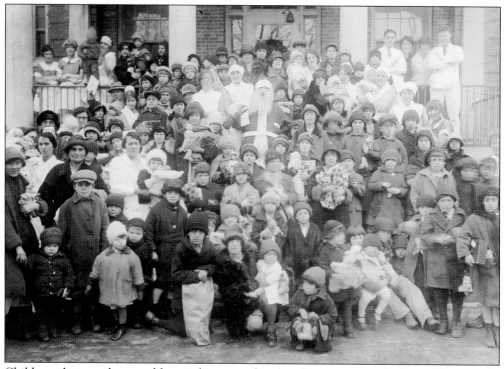

Children, their mothers, and hospital personnel gather for a picture with Santa Claus on the steps of the Lynn Hospital, *c.* 1915. (Courtesy of the Atlanticare Hospital.)

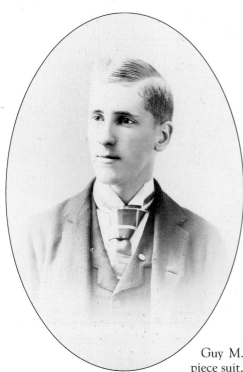

Guy M. Newhall, looking quite "dapper" in his three-piece suit, poses for his picture in 1894.

The fame and athletic skills of Harry Agganis, "The Golden Greek," are still remembered and recognized today. After leading the Lynn Classical football team to many victories in the 1940s, he went on to Boston University football, where he left B.U. grid records that are still intact. Harry was the Cleveland Browns #1 draft choice as a junior, but surprised all when he left football to play for the Boston Red Sox at a reportedly smaller salary. His sudden and untimely death in 1955 brought over twenty thousand people to pay their respects at St. George's Church and Pine Grove Cemetery. (Courtesy of the St. George Greek Orthodox Church.)

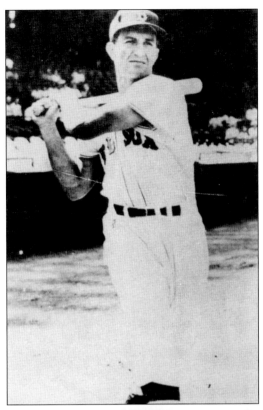

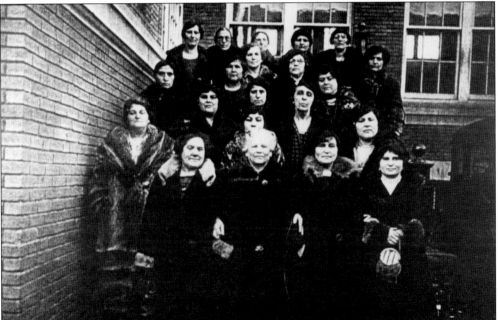

An Americanization class in 1938 at Washington School on Blossom Street. The first woman on the left, in the raccoon coat, is the mother of Rose Newman Levine. (Courtesy of the North Shore Jewish Historical Society.)

ACKNOWLEDGMENTS

I would like to thank all the people who helped to make this book a reality. Help has come from many different sources: friends and co-workers gave time and information, loaned books, and shared family pictures. In particular, Janice Bacon and Roger Tinkham started me off with my first pictures; Dave Comeau and Jeff Losano were especially helpful in gathering pictures for me; and Fred Cole's assistance with ideas and contacts was much appreciated. Many thanks are in order to Atlanticare Hospital for the use of many wonderful pictures of the old Lynn Hospital, which are especially important now, at a time when the hospital will soon be a thing of the past.

There are many people in the community who graciously took time to share pictures and information and to tell wonderful tales of bygone days. Special thanks to Jack Imperial at the mayor's office, Bob Matthias of the Lynn GAR, Wayne Livermore of the Mt. Carmel Lodge, the St. Stephens Episcopal and St. Georges Greek Orthodox Churches, and the librarians at both the Lynn English and Classical High Schools. At the Lynn Public Library, Nadine and her aides, with never a complaint, helped me search for pictures as I became a familiar face there. Additional thanks to Lil Limon of the North Shore Jewish Historical Society and to Calantha Sears of the Nahant Historical Society, as well as the Saugus Public Library, the Milford, NH Historical Society, and the Milford, NH Public Library. The Peabody Essex Museum Library in Salem was most helpful, as was the Newburyport Public Library.

David Carpenter, the General Electric Co. historian and author of the recent book *River Works History: A City Within a City*, has graciously allowed me to use pictures from his book.

The generous assistance of Brother Arcadius of St. John's Prep in Danvers, with Lynn church and city history, was most appreciated. Brother Arcadius is himself a native of Lynn. A very special thanks to Hugh McCarthy for his help and encouragement with my "book project," and for always knowing where to look for pictures. And last, but not least, I thank my family for their patience and willingness to adjust their schedules to mine.